The Churches in Europe as Witnesses to Healing

Keith Clements

**With a foreword by
Archbishop Anastasios
of Tirana, Durrës and All Albania**

WCC Publications, Geneva

Founded in 1948, the World Council of Churches is now a fellowship of more than 340 Christian churches confessing together "the Lord Jesus Christ according to the scriptures" and seeking "to fulfil together their common calling to the glory of the one God, Father, Son and Holy Spirit". Tracing its origins to international movements dedicated to world mission and evangelism, faith and order, life and work, church unity and Christian education, the World Council is made up primarily of Protestant and Orthodox churches. The Roman Catholic Church is not a member church but participates with the WCC and its member communions in a variety of activities and dialogues.

Cover design: Rob Lucas

ISBN 2-8254-1382-8

© 2003 WCC Publications
World Council of Churches
150 route de Ferney, P.O. Box 2100
1211 Geneva 2, Switzerland
Website: http://www.wcc-coe.org

Printed in Switzerland

The Churches
in Europe
as Witnesses
to Healing

Table of Contents

Foreword

The many challenging issues of our day confront not only theologians but all responsible Christians: peace-making in the world; overcoming violence and hatred; the role of the churches in a pluralistic, post-modern society; cooperation between Christians and the need for unity; ecumenicity as the rediscovery of our mutual interdependence, fellowship and spirituality; the relations between a particular identity and universal community; Europe's own need and responsibility for healing and reconciliation within its own frontiers and in relation to the entire world.

Very few church leaders deal competently with these crucial concerns in such a responsible, lucid and creative way as the author of this book. Keith Clements is particularly well equipped to handle these issues due to his long experience of ministry, his solid biblical and theological formation, his faith and commitment, his spiritual sensitivity and his critical thinking. The papers and meditations in this volume offer a powerful witness to the healing which is found in the love of God in Christ as it touches the lives of people in our time, both individually and collectively. I am deeply thankful that Dr Clements is making his thinking, convictions and vision available to a wider audience than those who were privileged to read or hear them the first time.

The texts in this volume, full of biblical insights and eloquently written, will offer to every Christian struggling with the problems of our time – irrespective of church affiliation – a new opportunity for inspiration and theological enrichment. There is so much in this book which can challenge and instruct us if we are humble enough to listen. Within its pages I read and hear the words of a dear friend and brother in Christ. They stimulate and challenge me, and encourage me to learn more of what the love of Christ and the mission of the church mean today. As such, they are to be received in profound gratitude.

My warm commendation of this book is accompanied by my humble prayers that it will enrich the thinking and the faith of many people in Europe and indeed of the whole oikoumene, and that the author's continuing service to the ecumenical movement will continue to be guided by the Holy Spirit and will bring forth "a hundredfold fruit".

At the beginning of the new millennium, Christians are called to renewed thinking and energy for reconciliation and creative co-existence in the world. We need vision and dynamic action instead of accepting passively an economic globalization which leads to the exploitation of peoples. We are called to struggle for a worldwide community of solidarity based on freedom, understanding and respect for one another, and most especially on the love revealed in the person of Christ, the Alpha and Omega of creation and history, upon whom we gaze in confidence.

Archbishop Anastasios
of Tirana, Durrës and All Albania

Introduction

The genesis of this book lay in conversations with the late Jan Kok, director of Publications at the World Council of Churches, a year or so before his untimely death in 2002. Jan encouraged me in the idea of writing a short book which would be relevant to the 12th assembly of the Conference of European Churches (CEC), to take place in Trondheim, Norway, in June 2003 on the theme "Jesus Christ Heals and Reconciles – Our Witness in Europe". But more than that, we hoped that it could also contribute to thinking on the wider scene where the churches are increasingly aware that their witness is to healing, wholeness and fullness of life in a broken world.

Eventually I began to reflect on the papers I had written or delivered, or sermons I had preached, in the five years since taking office in CEC, and found it was striking how, without any conscious forethought, so many of them had already focused on the calling of the churches to witness to healing and reconciliation. At first I felt a necessity to work up such materials into what might claim to be a more sustained or even systematic treatment of these themes. It was not, however, simply the pressures of work in a general secretary's office which made me decide to leave them as they are. Rather, it was the feeling of wanting to make clear that "ecumenical commitment" is at heart a matter of deeply personal faith and witness, and not an exercise in academic abstractions and ecclesiastical engineering.

Therefore I make no apology for the fact that, because most of these pieces were written for and delivered at a wide variety of occasions and places in many different parts of Europe, there is a variety of style and little sign of a developed argument running from first to last page, nor even an exact chronological order followed. Sometimes changes of mood may be detected (as congregations may experience with their pastor Sunday by Sunday!), not least in the sermons delivered from one year to the next at the annual Week of Prayer for Christian Unity. But "ad hockery", as it is sometimes called, also has its strengths and sometimes it is precisely the sparks which fly between faith and very specific contexts of time and place which travel furthest.

In most cases, the significance of the particular contexts should be clear, but perhaps some background features require a little more filling in. Several of the sermons given in 1999 refer to the Kosovo conflict and the way in which we in CEC, with other ecumenical partners, were engaged in accompanying the Serbian Orthodox Church, and other churches in Yugoslavia, through that fraught situation, to the extent of visiting Belgrade during the NATO military intervention. There were in fact two ecumenical visits in which I participated during those weeks, on 17-18 April and 27-28 May, the latter one including a meeting with the then president of Yugoslavia, Slobodan Milosevic.

Then in relation to the final sermon, preached in Georgia, the context is one in which acts of physical violence and destruction have been carried out against Protestant and Catholic communities by a renegade group claiming to be "Orthodox" but disowned by the Georgian Orthodox Church. Sadly, it has to be recorded that in January 2003, seven months after that sermon was preached there, the ecumenical service being held in the Baptist church in Tbilisi for the Week of Prayer for Christian Unity was violently broken up by that same group, dramatically underlining the fact that in some contexts in Europe even the most basic ecumenical witness can still be costly.

Without apology, though perhaps with a note of justification, I readily admit that in the pages which follow some of my own sources of inspiration are very apparent in the figures I refer to as exemplars of what Christian mission and witness are all about. Two in particular feature conspicuously on a number of pages: Dietrich Bonhoeffer and J.H. Oldham. The former has been a special subject of interest for me over many years, while the latter is the only figure whose biography I have written, and am ever likely to write. But it should not be assumed that these are the only people whom I consider to have anything important to say. They are just two among the great cloud of witnesses, and it so happens that they have spoken to me in my time and place. But I hope it will be just as evident that many other people and communities, some well-known and others misleadingly called "ordinary", have also been inspirational.

Now let me anticipate a remark which I know will be made in reaction to some of these pieces – because it has been made already by some who heard one or other of them "live". It is that on occasion I have painted somewhat too bleak a picture of the situation of Christianity, humanly speaking, in contemporary Europe. Maybe I have, although without the inspiring experience of meeting with so many Christians and churches all over Europe, some of them serving and witnessing with joy and courage in the grimmest of situations, these years with CEC would not have given me so much enrichment. But the *witness* of the church is not to itself and its achievements but to Jesus Christ, and the calling of the *preacher* is to point the congregation not to immediate worldly signs of hope but to the fundamental ground of hope and security, the faithfulness of God who will not let that witness be in vain. Only on that basis can the question be truly answered, "Are we still of any use?"

As always, there are acknowledgments to be made and thanks expressed. Two of the pieces, "The Churches of Europe: 'Are We Still of Any Use?'" and "On Being Prayed For", were first published in *International Review of Mission* (July 2002) and *The Ecumenical Review* (January-April 2002) respectively, and reappear here by kind permission of the editors of those journals. "Healing the Wound: A Return to China with Bonhoeffer" is a slightly modified version of an essay contributed to the Festschrift for Burton F. Nelson, *Reflections on Bonhoeffer* (Covenant Publications, Chicago, 1999), and I am grateful to the publisher and to the editors of the volume, Geoffrey Kelly and C. John Weborg, for their encouragement to reproduce it here. In Geneva, Irmheld Reichen-Young devoted much time and care to retrieving the texts from a variety of diskettes and hard copies, while to staff of WCC Publications gratitude is due for seeing this volume through the publication process so effectively and speedily.

Finally, it moves me more than I can say that His Beatitude Anastasios, head of the Orthodox Church of Albania, has kindly written a foreword. It would be enough to say that Archbishop Anastasios, to so many of us in Europe and also the wider world, is a superlative contemporary embodiment of witness to healing and reconciliation. But more than that, on a personal level he has in a rather special way been a pastor to me. In 2000 I was diagnosed as having a life-threatening illness which, thanks to surgical skill and subsequent treatment and by the healing grace of God, was averted so that I have been able to continue to live and work these further years to the full. By his prayerful interest and quiet solicitude on every occasion we have met or corresponded, Archbishop Anastasios has sought to convince me that even a general secretary can only live by grace and not by over-work, which is perhaps the most healing message of all. My wife Margaret, who has been trying to say the same thing for years, joins me in loving gratitude to him.

Keith Clements
Geneva, February 2003

The Churches of Europe: "Are We Still of Any Use?"

A very bright and engaging Norwegian woman Lutheran pastor recently arrived in Geneva to attend one of our Conference of European Churches (CEC) meetings. She told me that on the 'plane she had got into conversation with the businessman sitting next to her, and over the in-flight meal they had enquired about each other's work. The businessman was simply bemused and incredulous that any evidently intelligent person like his fellow passenger could still call herself an active Christian, let alone be a pastor. Many of us can no doubt recount similar experiences. It is not that our faith is attacked, or our activity criticized; they are simply seen as pointless, a useless irrelevance in the contemporary world.

If we are honest, we have to admit that such reaction is understandable. In many parts of Europe, active church attendance is in dramatic decline. Even more to the point, popular acquaintance with the Christian tradition is fast disappearing. A German colleague tells me that on a recent television quiz show, a pair of participants had to rearrange in the correct order the words (in their English equivalent) "Father", "heaven", "art", "our", "in", "which". They were unable to do so. In Denmark, a country which describes itself as Lutheran and where the great majority are still baptized as infants, I am told that a recent university survey showed that most students, even of religious studies, manifested more awareness of, and interest in, New Age-type beliefs in reincarnation than the Christian doctrine of *the* Incarnation. In much of our media, organized religion is seen patronizingly as an esoteric concern of an obsolescent minority, and especially, as far as public and political life goes, is viewed as at best irrelevant, and at worst a dangerous intrusion. In Britain, Prime Minister Tony Blair's Christianity, even his declared debt to Christian socialism, is mocked by, of all people, a *Guardian* columnist, while the editor of the German weekly *Der Spiegel* declares that the churches have no role in the public life of the new Europe.

Again, if we are honest, we can understand why religion is seen as a dangerous virus rather than a healthy ingredient in society. Look at the religious factor, say our cultured despisers, in conflicts everywhere from

Northern Ireland to the former Yugoslavia, from the Middle East to Sri Lanka. This is a reaction that is even more marked since the events of 11 September 2001. The situation seems no different at the highest level of decision-making in the most potent force for change in contemporary Europe, viz. the European Union (EU). In November 2000 at the Nice summit, the heads of EU governments adopted a charter of fundamental rights. While the right to *individual* belief and conscience was recognized, the specific contribution of religious *communities* to the life and culture of Europe was expressly excluded.

The scene is not wholly encouraging in the post-communist East. Revival of Christian life is evident in some quarters. However, ten years after the fall of communism, there is no wholesale evidence of a popular resurgence of Christianity to fill the vacuum left by the departure of state atheism. An evangelical leader in Romania recently confided to me that his denomination was now in a process of serious reflection on why the great hoped-for evangelistic breakthrough had not occurred in the decade after the fall of Ceaucescu.

How to respond?

Europe today therefore seems in many respects a bleak climate for the churches. Christians are on the margins of much of European life. Characteristic official responses from the churches to this situation are of three kinds.

1. Denial: Official church spokesmen (yes, they usually are men) can be heard declaiming that the position is not nearly so bad, especially for the national and established churches. The old order is intact. In Britain one still hears this from some Anglican bishops (and some of my best friends are Anglican bishops): the national church is here for all the people, and deep down there is respect for the church as the unifying guardian of national values. This is largely self-delusion. For one thing, what is often claimed to be the specific role of the Church of England as a body concerned for the whole of public life, making it different from a "mere sect", is no less true today for the free churches and the Roman Catholic Church in Britain, all of which see themselves as endowed with responsibility in the public sphere. For another thing, there are whole swathes of the population, of various faiths and none, in whose consciousness the church, be it Anglican or any other denomination, plays no practical role.

Such efforts at self-delusion are not peculiar to Britain, however. At a Europe regional meeting during the World Council of Churches (WCC) central committee at Potsdam in February 2001, I suggested that we have to recognize that "Christendom" is now dead. I was thoroughly taken to task for this comment by a Greek Orthodox professor (who is also a good friend of mine). By "Christendom" I meant the old alliance between church and state, that hand-in-glove relationship which once upon a time ensured national stability and a society of uniform values.

2. Introversion: Since we can no longer dominate or control a society which is bewilderingly secular and pluralist by turns, a second response says we should turn away from this society and create our own within the Christian fold. It is a widespread temptation: to opt for the cultivation of a spirituality and social life divorced from the messy and threatening world outside.

3. Aggressive restorationism: In a third response there is a conscious attempt to gain or regain control of society by direct access to political power. There are appearing in Britain, I am told, some versions of the fundamentalist evangelicalism more familiar in the USA, which seeks power through control of a political party. In Italy, the Protestant minorities are very wary of attempts by some circles in the Roman Catholic Church to wield direct political control in an attempt to stem the inexorable movement towards a religiously and ethnically pluralist society.

Denial, introversion and aggressive restorationism are inadequate responses to a critical situation. It is not simply that history will prove them to be futile for the future of Christianity in Western society. They do not help us to answer the question, "Are we still of any use?" because, in fact, they are not really daring to face that question in all the starkness of our context. Still more fundamentally, they are out of keeping with the nature of the gospel that is good news for the world, the gospel of God's free and costly grace for all humankind. They are not missionary. They know little of Pentecost.

Are we still of any use?

"Are we still of any use?" It sounds a despairing question, but it need not be. I have lifted this question from an essay written during the winter of 1942-43 by Dietrich Bonhoeffer, in the midst of war and his involvement in the German resistance.[1] He wrote the piece as a present for his relatives and close friends who were also taking part in the resistance. It is a reflection on their common experience of struggle, anxiety and suffering during the previous few years. But it is also a forward-looking, future-oriented reflection in which he defends the attitude of optimism. Bonhoeffer raises the question "Are we still of any use?" having spoken of what participation in political conspiracy has done ethically for his circle. They have had to learn "the arts of equivocation and pretence". The need to remain hidden within the totalitarian system in order to survive and eventually strike a blow to bring it down "has made us suspicious of others and kept us from being truthful and open". But then Bonhoeffer looks forward to a post-Hitler time: "What we shall need is not geniuses, or cynics, or misanthropes, or clever tacticians, but plain, honest, straightforward people." He is looking forward to the time of rebuilding national and Christian life in Germany. He is hoping that he and his comrades will be there to take part in it. But they will have to learn a new way of life, and values other than those of resisters will have to take priority. It is not, though, that everything they have experienced and learnt will now be irrelevant: "There remains an experience of incomparable value. We have for once learnt to see the great events of world history from below, from the perspective of the outcast, the suspects, the maltreated, the powerless, the opposed, the reviled – in short, from the perspective of those who suffer." That, says Bonhoeffer, is what the resisters must preserve and carry forward as part of their faith for the next phase of their history.

Bonhoeffer's situation and ours are very different. However, I would like us to adopt the *spirit* of what Bonhoeffer is saying as Christians and churches, and ask, "Are we still of any use?" in the new Europe that is emerging. We may describe this new Europe in many ways: the post-Christian Europe, the post-imperialist Europe, the post-modern Europe, the secularized Europe, the religiously pluralist Europe, the democratizing Europe, the integrating Europe, or whatever. However we describe it, it is a confused and confusing Europe, and one in which institutional Christianity is on the margins. What are the transformations we have to undergo in order to engage with it? Also, what is there from our past and present experience, however negative that may seem at first sight, which can help us be truly part of the next phase of history? How can we face realities in a spirit of hope, and a belief in ourselves as having a vital role to play?

A new calling to mission

I feel encouraged in this because I believe a new sense of calling to mission within their own continent is apparent within many of the European churches just now, and moreover within CEC as well. In fact, for some years common mission in Europe has been a subject of study for us. I would commend the report of our consultation held at Bad Herrenalb, Germany, in 2001: *Giving an Account of the Hope Within Us – the Common Call of the European Churches to Mission.*[2] The next (12th) CEC assembly, to take place at Trondheim, Norway, in 2003, has as its theme "Jesus Christ Heals and Reconciles – Our Witness in Europe". This is the first time that witness, and witness to Jesus Christ himself, have been so explicitly stated in a CEC assembly theme. Not only is this

so, but there is now the "Charta Oecumenica: Guidelines for the Growing Cooperation among the Churches in Europe", drawn up by CEC and
the Council of European Bishops' Conferences, and transmitted to all the
European churches from the Ecumenical Encounter in Strasbourg just
after Easter 2001.[3] The first draft of this "Charta" was put out to all the
churches in 1999 for more than a year of discussion and feedback. In the
feedback, it was striking that one of the points most often stressed, from
Protestants, Orthodox and Catholics alike, was the need for a stronger
missiological note to be sounded. So now we read at the very beginning
of the second section, "On the Way Towards the Visible Fellowship of
the Churches in Europe":

> The most important task of the churches in Europe is the common proclama-
> tion of the gospel, in both word and deed, for the salvation of all... This wit-
> ness will require increased dedication to Christian education... and pastoral
> care in local congregations, with a sharing of experiences in these fields. It is
> equally important for the whole people of God to communicate the gospel in
> the public domain, which also means responsible commitments to social and
> political issues.

In CEC itself, we are hoping soon to establish a consultancy on ecumenical mission in Europe. It is encouraging, too, that not least in
Britain fresh attention is being given to missiology. An example of this
is the most provocative and useful symposium report produced in 2001
by Churches Together in Britain and Ireland, *Christian Mission in Western Society*.[4] At the European level, I would also strongly commend the
manifesto produced by the European Methodist Theological Commission in 1998, *Christ Before Us*.

A biblical perspective

Presently, I would like to offer suggestions of four areas in which I
believe that we as Christians and churches engaged in mission can be of
use in the future development of Europe, a Europe of justice and peace,
and alive to God. But first, a short biblical excursus for the sake of some
basic orientation. Let us look briefly at the end of the gospel of Luke,
and the beginning of the Acts of the Apostles. These are among those
passages in the New Testament which have always been inspirational for
the Christian mission in the world.

Luke 24:44-49: The risen Jesus, after opening the apostles' minds to
understand the scriptural testimony to him, his suffering and rising from
the dead, and saying that repentance and forgiveness of sins is to be proclaimed in his name to all nations, declares: "You are witnesses of these
things. And see, I am sending upon you what my Father promised; so

stay here in the city until you have been clothed with power from on high." And then he is taken up into heaven.

Acts 1:6-8: This is part of Luke's second account of the ascension.

> So when (the apostles) had come together, they asked him, "Lord, is this the time when you will restore the kingdom to Israel?" He replied, "It is not for you to know the times or periods that the Father has set by his own authority. But you will receive power when the Holy Spirit has come upon you; and you will be my witnesses in Jerusalem, in all Judaea and Samaria, and to the ends of the earth."

Note carefully that in the first passage: "You are witnesses of these things"; and in the second, "You will be my witnesses" are not commands or exhortations "to be" my witnesses. Here it is indicative, not imperative. We have a simple statement of fact, and a promise. The promise is based on the promise of the Spirit, which will clothe them with power – power to be witnesses. In the second passage, the apostles have asked Jesus about the restoration of political power and sovereignty. Jesus tells them this is an unanswerable question and one which does not concern them. They will simply be witnesses; they will not be able to be anything other than witnesses. Nothing more, and nothing less, in the power of the Spirit.

This is surely liberating! The messengers of Jesus are not to demoralize and cripple themselves by imposing on themselves unfulfillable dreams and ambitions. In the power of the Spirit, the apostles will just be witnesses to what God has done and will do through the suffering, death and resurrection of Jesus, and to the new life of forgiveness and reconciliation through him. They are to go to the ends of the earth, but are not to set themselves the task of conquering the world or attempting to control it. The future destiny of the world and the end of history are not in their hands, but God's. They will be witnesses, nothing more, nothing less. In *that* mission, they are both free and unstoppable.

The word used for "witnesses" in the Greek text is *martures*. Before long, the early church gave a special meaning to this word: those who witnessed to the point of surrendering their lives, the "martyrs". We should not limit "witnessing" to "martyrdom" but it is a poignant reminder that witness to Jesus is not just a matter of words, but of what we do with our lives in the face of the powers of this present age. The Spirit can use weakness and suffering at least as much as apparent success.

With this basic biblical orientation, let us now look at some areas where, as those engaged in Christian mission in Europe, we can certainly be "of use" in the development of a Europe of justice and peace, and alive to God. Let us look not for unfulfillable ambitions but for places and manageable tasks which can provide points of witness.

European unity

First, I want to consider the unity of Europe. Politically and economically, Europe is on the way to some sort of integration. The most powerful motor in this process is the European Union. At present there are 15 member states but with a queue of applicant countries waiting. These include Poland, the Czech Republic, Hungary and Slovenia, with more in the list of hopefuls. We should not forget, however, the equally important and already pan-European institutions such as the Council of Europe and the Organization for Security and Cooperation in Europe. I say "some sort of" integration because whatever die-hard Eurosceptics in Britain may say, far from any single, coherent blueprint for the future of Europe being drawn up in Brussels, there is as yet no agreement among the EU member governments about the course by which the European ship is to sail. The most that can be said is that a public debate is being launched and that 2004 will be a crucial year of decision about the future size and shape of the EU.

But some sort of integration involving the word "federalism" is before us. I do not see how any Christian mind can be opposed to this in principle. We are gloriously privileged to live in a time of opportunity for Europe to overcome both the divisions which have plagued it in the past, and which have generated devastating wars for itself from the 17th century onwards, and the rivalries that, moreover, have been exported with tragic consequences for the rest of the world, especially in Africa and Asia, right through the colonial and imperialist age to the cold-war period. Moreover, we should always remember that Jean Monnet and Robert Schumann, the founding fathers of what has become the EU, were imbued with a profoundly Christian vision. They had a concept of a new political and economic order in Europe, especially in the relations between France and Germany, which would make war not only undesirable but also impossible.

The churches as institutions of Christianity might seem to be on the margins. But being on the margins does not mean that we and the political decision-makers are out of earshot of each other. Moreover, it is also a fact that many of those at the centre of the European project in Brussels and Strasbourg, far from being "faceless bureaucrats", are deeply exercised about the whole question of the moral and spiritual *values* – the "soul" – which must undergird a united Europe, whatever outward form that unity takes, and animate the body politic and economic. At the CEC central committee meeting in Iasi, Romania, in October 2000, we spent a whole day on the subject of "A Search for Common European Values – the Role of the Churches".[5] It was a dialogue with a Romanian government minister and a senior executive of the European Parliament. It is a dialogue which continues through our ecumenical presence in Brussels and Strasbourg, with our CEC Commission on Church and Society and the Roman Catholic equivalent, the Commission of the Bishops Conferences of the European Union. These are instruments through which a positive yet critical dialogue is established with the European decision-making process on issues ranging from the economic and social consequences of former communist countries joining the EU, to environmental care; from the new security architecture of Europe, to bio-ethics; and from north-south trade, to human rights. Here, we offer our witness which centres on the question to which all economic and political debate eventually points: "What does it mean to be human?"

A united Europe means a commonwealth of values, as well as a common political and economic order. To that, Christians and churches have a vital contribution to make. But it goes further than that. Why is European unity so elusive as an idea and a fact? How do common values come into currency? Europe is peculiar in that it already has so much of a heritage in common, and a history which has bound us together in weal and woe. Yet, it is also a collection of communities which still seem so opaque to each other. It is a region of intimate connections and no less of mutual suspicions, even in the western part, let alone between East and West.

A united Europe, a Europe at peace, will only be possible if we find a way of accepting and appreciating our diversities of culture as belonging together and enriching each other. Here is where the ecumenical witness is vital. I do not see ecumenism as the attempt to reach a uniformity of church structure and authority. It is rather the effort to identify and recognize the presence of the one Christ, and the catholicity of faith in one another's traditions, however diverse. Our "Charta Oecumenica" will, I hope, be seen as an aid in this attempt.

My own hope and prayer is that in my life-time I may at least see eucharistic hospitality, if not actual intercommunion, become the practice for all churches, Protestant, Roman Catholic and Orthodox alike. Even that will not have real meaning if there is not also a project for intercommunion in the Holy Spirit. By this, I mean the willingness for us to enter into a deep empathy with the ethos, the history and the theology of the other tradition. This will mean sitting where the other sits, and imagining ourselves into the particular national and religious historical experience which has made the others what they are. Above all, we need to stand and pray where the others pray, and empathize with how they pray. Nicholas Sagovsky, in his recent splendid study of ecumenism as communion or koinonia, argues that in both the New Testament and the church fathers it is communion as a way of *life* reflecting that of the Holy Trinity which predominates over dogma: "What this means for the church can only be spelt out in terms of a practice which incorporates a doctrine, not a doctrine from which a practice can be derived."[6]

This process of indwelling in the life of the other takes time and patience; it takes spiritual discipline. Let me give an example from my own experience. As a Western born and bred and theologically educated Protestant, it has taken me a long time to really appreciate what is happening in Orthodox worship. By nurture and education, I was imbued with the belief that in the normal act of Sunday worship we begin with praise to God, invocation of the Holy Spirit and confession of our sins, and then proceed to hear the word of God through the reading of the scriptures and preaching from it. Then we move to prayers of intercession for the world and our own needs, with the whole culminating preferably in the act of communion followed by a dismissal to go and be good Christians in the world. Worship, on this understanding, is *linear*. It is like a train journey on a straight line with a beginning, middle and end: perfectly rational and logical.

Frequently Westerners at first find Orthodox worship, for all its grand visual and choral beauty, not only exhaustingly long but grossly repetitious, with endless *kyrie eleisons*, and extracts from the psalms and ascriptions of praise in seemingly random order. It was while attending a particularly strenuous service of vespers in an Orthodox monastery in Finland that the penny finally dropped for me. This was not linear worship but *circular*: a ceaseless procession *around* the altar. Not so much the sparrow flying in a straight line from tree to tree, but the eagle soaring and circling, and drawing up all creation into the heavenly worship. Such circular procession is as valid a response to the glory and inexhaustible wonder of God as Western linear worship. I continue to worship as a Western Protestant, but with an awareness of another dimension that I find marvellously enriching.

All this might seem a far cry from the question of the unity of Europe. But true unity requires that people enter into the place of the other and learn from it, however strange that place might appear to be. This is a witness to and a way of being Christ, who entered into our place, ultimately on the cross, to create the one new human being in place of Jew and Gentile, slave and free, Greek and barbarian, male and female. This underlines the importance of building bridges between churches of diverse confessions and in very different locations in Europe. It is impossible to build true partnerships between congregations without also entering into the social and cultural milieus in which they live. We can witness to what being European today requires by setting examples of mutual learning about each other's religious, national, political and cultural contexts. This, of course, has big implications for interfaith relations as well.

Peace-making

Second, I will consider peace-making as an area where we can be "of use" in the development of a Europe of justice and peace, and alive to God. Notwithstanding all that can be said about religion being a factor in generating or exacerbating conflict, faith communities can and do play a role in reconciliation. That is not just a wishful idea or argument on my part, but a fact. I would like to have placed on every EU commissioner's desk, and in every foreign ministry official's hands, the recent study by Scott Appleby, *The Ambivalence of the Sacred: Religion, Violence and Reconciliation.*[7] It is a thorough, wide-ranging and painstaking assessment of the work done by religious peace-making groups and individuals, Christians and others, around the world in the past twenty years. It is, above all, fair. On the one hand, Appleby not only faces squarely the way religious fundamentalism often seeks to justify violence, he also exposes the double-talk which churches indulge in when they try to distance themselves from violent conflict which has a religious element. "This is not a religious war," we hear said from Northern Ireland to the Balkans and Chechnya. "We are for peace; religion is being misused and exploited for political purposes." But as Appleby notes, church leaders rarely ask why their brand of religion has become so easily exploitable in the first place. How does it come about that, at a popular level, and largely through a lack of education about what their faith means, masses of people view their religious affiliation simply as a badge of communal identity rather than as a commitment to a specific way of life defined in moral and spiritual terms?

On the other hand, Appleby makes equally clear that, again and again in all kinds of faith traditions, we also find those who discern at the core of their faith a commitment to the non-violent resolution of conflicts and reconciliation. These are people who, in that commitment, are able to transcend the limits of national, ethnic and sectarian loyalty. Sometimes such a person is a prominent church leader in the public eye. Europe is not without its parallels with the Desmond Tutus and Beyers Naudés of South Africa. I think for example of the head of the Orthodox Church of Albania, Archbishop Anastasios, who has a vision of all peoples and tribes and tongues in the Balkans learning to live together without fear. This is not only a vision. When two years ago Kosovar Albanian refugees, nearly all Muslims of course, flooded into Albania, Anastasios told the students at his Orthodox seminary in Durrës to shut their books and go into the camps with food parcels and medical supplies. "But", said some of the students, "after their experiences under the Serbs, they hate us Orthodox. They will want to kill us." "Well, show them Orthodox love," said the archbishop. And they went, and those they helped have never forgotten them.

High-profile organizations like the World Conference on Religion and Peace, and the Sant'Egidio Community, as well as ecumenical bodies like the WCC and even CEC, can justly claim to have taken important initiatives at mediation during conflicts, for maintaining dialogue between parties, and for encouraging the rebuilding of fractured relationships when the actual fighting stops. No less important is the role of lesser-known individuals and small, informal groups, often acting anonymously, who act as bridge-builders. Northern Ireland provides many instances. Being an effective mediator means having a measure of independence from the conflict, yet being immersed in its issues. It means staying free of the pressure to take sides, yet bearing the pain of both sides and enabling each party to discover how things appear in the eyes of the other. It means waiting patiently in the darkness of the situation, yet with the hope that light will dawn. It is to be in a situation yet not conditioned by it. It seems that it is precisely a faith in God, and a belief in a reality that transcends the issues and parties in a conflict, and is graciously turned towards its healing, which motivates, liberates and strengthens people for such work.

Now, of course, it may well be said that in being involved in such work, churches and Christians and other religious people are doing no more than paying their dues, since it is religion in the first place which has been a factor in the disputes. It is certainly true that the first contribution by the churches to the healing of Europe must be greater reconciliation and unity among themselves. But, when it comes down to it, religion as such is only one element. The conflicts are so often about the recognition of the human rights of minorities, or about experiences of economic deprivation and exploitation, yet not even these alone. So often these are entangled with the ideologies and rhetoric of national or ethnic loyalty, which in turn are enmeshed in the memories, stories and myths, the fact and the fiction, which make up a community's remembered history. Europe is a bundle of versions of history. Some go back decades, some several centuries, and all find outlets in the behaviour of the individual men and women whose mind-sets they govern. It is these histories and memories which need healing and reconciliation, as shown, for example, by the work of the Irish School of Ecumenics, which we are seeking to take up in CEC at a European level, especially in south-east Europe.[8]

Secular governments and international bodies have their own vital role to play in the reconstruction of life in the aftermath of conflict. This is well seen in the cooperation of the EU and the Stability Pact for South-East Europe in providing funding for rebuilding the economy and much of the social life wrecked by war in the former Yugoslavia. Such reconstruction is a necessary condition for reconciliation, but not a *sufficient* condition. Reconciliation means alienated parties freely accepting each other into a new relationship and partnership. That cannot be programmed or guaranteed by finance. It comes through ventures of trust that involve risk: the risk of sharing one's version of the truth as one has perceived it, and the risk of hearing the truth as the other has experienced it. It can involve the costly risk of offering forgiveness to the other, and maybe the even more costly recognition that we ourselves need the forgiveness of the other. But "forgiveness" often sounds an embarrassing word, cosily religious or sloppily sentimental. Outside the Bible and the liturgy, it seems to belong only in romantic novels. What place does it have in the public and political realm?

Duncan Forrester tells an interesting story about his work on theology and public issues in Edinburgh, Scotland. At one of his working groups on criminal justice, an experienced woman prison governor – a committed Christian – sat silent through long discussions of the standard theories of criminal justice and punishment.

> None of them seemed to fit reality or give adequate guidance for practice. Then she said, quite quietly, that she had two rather different primary concerns. The first was that in the prison system today so few people were willing to face up to guilt, or respond to it in any serious way. Her second concern was with forgiveness and reconciliation. Few people, she said, regard the criminal system and prisons in particular as having anything to do with forgiveness – indeed, they tend to assume that forgiveness and mercy are the contrary of justice.[9]

Far from being an embarrassingly pious intrusion, this became the turning point of the whole discussion, which was now lifted on to a new plane. The group felt compelled to affirm that forgiveness, reconciliation, and reception back into fellowship were the goal and end of punishment without which a system of criminal justice lacks moral credibility. Christian insight had become public truth.

Forgiveness, instead of being confined to private piety, must be enabled to become public property in the life of peoples and nations. "Repentance and forgiveness of sins is to be proclaimed to all nations"

– and all national life. There is our witness. If we do not give it, who will?

An inclusive community

Third, Christians can be "of use" in their witness to the need of Europe to be a truly inclusive community. If Christians and churches feel themselves to be on the margins of much European life, rather than that being a tragedy to be lamented, it could be the point at which we discover our real vocation for our time, just as Bonhoeffer felt that for his circle "the view from below" might be their most precious acquisition. Rather than encouraging us to bemoan our own fate, it might enable us to empathize much more readily with those people and communities who are far more marginalized than we are, and for whom we can be a voice. Many of us in Western Europe will acknowledge that it was the great struggle against apartheid in South Africa, and being able to share in it in some way, which in turn conscientized us to the racism in our own societies and in ourselves. We began to see the need, both as citizens and as churches, for a new relationship and partnership with the black and Asian communities in our own country. We realized that the struggle for racial justice was as real here as in Soweto and Crossroads. That commitment now has to be extended to the refugees and asylum-seekers coming to Western Europe, including Britain, who are the targets of brutal xenophobic hostility from certain politicians and sections of the media. Europe can only be a healthy society if it is open to all in need, and whose expectations of just and humane reception can be met.

That commitment needs to be extended still further. It is only quite recently that the situation of what might be called indigenous European minorities, in our midst but marginalized for centuries, is being highlighted. I refer particularly to the Roma, Sinti and Sami people. For some time now, we in CEC have had a concern for Roma communities, especially in Eastern and Central Europe. In October 2001 our central committee, at its meeting in Romania, called for European churches to establish links with Roma communities, not least because there are many Roma Christians of all confessions, and to devote a special Sunday in the year to remembering them. Why is their situation so critical? It is not simply that their culture seems to be so strange to the rest of us, and subject either to romanticization or stereotyped demonization. It is because, uniquely among all minorities in Europe, the Roma have no home country; there is no Roma government which, at the end of the day, will offer them refuge or plead their cause. Hungarian minorities in Romania and Yugoslavia at least have Hungary, Turks have Turkey, and Jewish people know there is a state of Israel. But the Roma have no state back home, and no embassies in the European capitals to whom they can look for support. They can only depend on the common commitment of European governments and peoples to the international standards of human rights which they, at least on paper, support.

It is hard to see any Europe-wide community other than the churches, who profess a belief in the God-given dignity of every human being, which can stand by communities such as the Roma. Interesting things happen when we, as churches, feeling relatively weak and powerless ourselves, seek solidarity with the powerless. We discover we do have a certain kind of power – for others. In May 2001 CEC and the Churches Commission for Migrants in Europe held a consultation in Bratislava, Republic of Slovakia, on the situation of Roma people in Central Europe, in relation to the human-rights standards of the Council of Europe, the Organization for Security and Cooperation in Europe and the EU. Slovakia is a country where the relations between Roma and the majority population are particularly fraught. Roma people themselves, from several countries in Europe, took part in the consultation. What surprised us was the eagerness of leading members of the Slovakian government to attend as well. We had respectfully invited them, and more came than were invited. Here the Roma found a space and opportunity for honest dialogue, which had hitherto been denied them. I find that a kind of parable for much of our witness in Europe today. Let us use our situation, which might seem to be marginal, to be an empowering opportunity for others. However marginal we might appear to be, we do also have access to the decision-makers in Brussels and Strasbourg, and the capitals of Europe, and that too we should use on behalf of the most disempowered. "You shall be clothed with power from on high" – not so much for yourselves, as for those really left on the side.

One could go on. Among the most vulnerable people in Europe today are the thousands of young women and girls trafficked from the East to the West and into sexual and other forms of slavery. The churches can share in the massive job of combating this evil through the education of people in the East, and the protection of victims who come to the West. When CEC held a consultation on the issue in Driebergen, The Netherlands, in December 1999, we discovered that it was precisely the nature of the Christian fellowship as a transnational network across Europe that can be mobilized for this. For example, it is the houses of religious orders, themselves part of a pan-European network, which are often ideally placed to receive and protect and help rehabilitate the victims back in their home countries. Old wineskins *can* sometimes find new and vital roles for the public good.[10]

That brings us back to a recurrent issue. If the church is to be an effective instrument for the healing of European society, it must itself become a community which exemplifies real equality between women and men, and overcome within itself the disparities and abuse of power which lie behind sexual exploitation and other forms of domination. I would like to think that our Ecumenical Encounter in Strasbourg 2001, to which I have already referred, was a modest attempt to set an example of true community. Here we had a meeting not only between the governing bodies of CEC and the Council of European Bishops' Conferences together with number of other invited church leaders, but there were also an equal number of young people present, women and men, from all confessions and all parts of Europe. It was not an ecumenical meeting to which the youth were also invited, nor a youth gathering at which church leaders were invited to make pronouncements to the young and "hand on" their vision of the future of the faith in Europe. It was meant to be a true encounter, on equal terms, between the generations. And it was. Young people testified to the seriousness and depth of their faith in Christ. Leaders, cardinals and bishops felt able to admit their vulnerability. Many, on both sides, said it was a uniquely renewing experience.

Life with a new meaning

Fourth, and at the risk of sounding banal, there is the question of the meaning of life. The churches of Europe, whatever else they may do or not do, will be of use only if they are able to invite people into a life which gives meaning, purpose and fulfilment beyond what is provided by mere consumerism, entertainment or even work itself – not to mention the new forms of asceticism (notice the new cult of "health" as an end in itself in our over-fed societies in the West). It has become almost a commonplace to remark that while active allegiance to institutional Christianity is in sharp decline, and moreover other world faiths are not making noticeable inroads into European society, surveys show that people at large are not uninterested in ethics and spirituality, and indeed many would describe themselves as searching for some kind of spiritual basis for their lives. It is tempting for churches to imagine that if they keep their doors open long enough the people will return, having given up on astrology, New Age and other varieties of do-it-yourself religion. But the anti-institutional instincts of our time run too deep for that to be a realistic hope, as many of us know even from our own children.

Two kinds of implicit despair at this situation are evident among some of those wrestling with what Christian mission means in Western society today. On the one hand, there are voices saying that Western culture has been so distorted and corrupted by the Enlightenment, with its rationalism, individualism and materialism, that it is completely impervious to biblical faith. European culture is no longer "gospel-friendly". Their question is, "Can Europe be saved?" And their answer is, "No, unless there is a radical transformation of this culture." The late Bishop Lesslie Newbigin, to whom many of us owe an immense theological and personal debt, is often invoked in support of this view.

This attitude I find uncongenial for several reasons. For one, it seems sheer fantasy to imagine that, even if it were desirable, we can first change a whole culture to suit our evangelism. As Werner Ustorf of Birmingham has said, it resembles the proverbial king who is rejected by his people and so asks his advisers to provide him with a new population.[11] Second, it assumes a God-like vantage point from which we mortals can pronounce the last judgment on a whole world (or at least a whole continent). Instead, we have to accept that European societies and cultures make up a muddled scene, with some gospel-unfriendly and some gospel-friendlier features, in which both secular and Christian products are mixed confusedly together. As well as individualism, there are irrepressible yearnings for community. As well as rationalism, there is a search for some kind of contact with the infinite. As well as trivialization, there is a subterranean longing for facing the mysteries of life and its ending.

On the other hand, I hear voices saying that the problem is not with European culture but rather with the traditional Christian belief in the uniqueness of Jesus Christ as God's saving revelation. It is asserted that this is no longer tenable in the religiously pluralist, post-modern world which has given up entirely on any single, grand meta-narrative as truth for all. In the post-modern age, truth is fragmentary, piecemeal by nature, and the Christian tradition can see itself as but one fragment.

This alternative makes me uneasy on other grounds. First, it seems to accept too readily the self-congratulation of post-modernism on having given up on "truth for all". I think I now know when I first encountered post-modernism. Several years ago my wife and I were having dinner in a Chinese restaurant in Liverpool, and could not help overhearing the conversation at the next table. A young man and a young woman were having what was evidently an early date in their relationship. The young man said, "I can't stand people who erudite." She asked, "What does that mean?" He replied, "Using words other people cannot understand." A long silence ensued. It is a silence which post-modernism is helpless to break, for it assumes that it is okay for there to be non-understanding between different cultures and discourses of belief.

Second, I am suspicious of its psychology. It appears to be more willing to defend the rights of other believers to their identities, than actually to identify with one's own tradition. At first that sounds a very liberal and enlightened recognition of plurality. In fact, it is self-contradictory and manifests what amounts to a self-hatred born out of an inability to cope with the insecurity of being on the margins. Unable to cope, it internalizes the contempt of the society by whom it feels rejected (one may compare this situation with one of the most tragic fruits of anti-semitism in 19th/20th-century Europe, viz. the self-denigration by some Jews of their own Jewishness).

The root question European people will go on asking is, "Who am I?" Many of them feel betrayed by the stock answers previously told them: "You are a member of the proletariat engaged in the great people's revolution"; "You are a child of a great nation which has suffered so much in the past and you must prove yourself worthy of your forbears' sacrifices by a like willingness to sacrifice today"; "You are a free individual in a free society, entitled to all your rights and to whatever you can achieve by your enterprise." Today, as it dawns on Europeans that in a globalized world they are members of a worldwide market economy, they are further being told, "You are a consumer, free to choose whatever you want from the new infinity of choices the global market offers you." There is a catch in this last answer: that some are freer than others to choose. Nicholas Boyle, a Cambridge liberal Catholic scholar, puts his finger right on the spot when he states that the real danger of the globalized economy lies in the way it deceives us into thinking of ourselves only as consumers with an infinite variety of choices, and denies us the truth that we live in a world of finite resources and that, moreover, through our work we are also called to be producers. That requires a new spiritual self-discipline of living with obligations and more modest material expectations:

> Recognizing ourselves as self-constraining consumer-producers we recognize not only our finitude but that of the world we inhabit. There is one world and it is not endless and we have to work out among ourselves how we are to live in it together or we shall die in it separately.[12]

If that is the hard reality out of which *good news* – gospel – for our time has to be wrought, then Christians and churches in Europe are of vital use. Believing in one who became human in one time and place among us, and in that incarnate particularity, which was a life of servanthood that culminated in a dreadful death, showed himself to be the way, the truth and the life, we have a faith that life can find its true fulfilment in accepting its particularities, its finitude, its being tied together with others, here and now. As one of the great fathers of the early church St Irenaeus put it, "The glory of God is a living human being, and the life of the human is to glorify God."

The question is *how* this faith is to be shared and witnessed to in Europe today. This is a Europe of people suspicious of institutions and tired of rhetoric, a people more interested in searching for their own answers than receiving prescriptions. To be conscious of being on the margins may be the best place to know and witness to a belief in the otherness, the strangeness of God, and the life of love God offers us. Can we not find ways in which people are accompanied in their searching, as on the Emmaus road, rather than simply being told what the destination is? Should we not admit that, more often than we care to acknowledge, our own faith did not come down as a ready-made package from heaven, but owed so much to our being given time and space to explore what Christ might mean to us, and that the exploration is still going on? That the opportunity for conversation was as significant as being preached to? And that being able to participate anonymously in occasions of worship was as important as direct confrontation? To quote Werner Ustorf again:

> What Christianity has to offer is a space where people get the chance to reconstruct themselves before God... This is an open space in which the absence and the suffering, the love and the otherness of God is experienced, generating the space for genuine history, for human freedom and for various ways of interpreting Christ.[13]

"Are we still of any use?" I have tried to affirm that this is not a despairing question but one that leads us to hope. As European churches, we may be on the margins compared with the churches of former times. But the margins can be a good place to be for rediscovering our usefulness, for the sake of the unity of Europe, for the sake of peace and reconciliation, for the sake of those disempowered, and for the sake of sharing the faith we own, and all of this for the sake of a Europe of justice and peace and alive to God. It is precisely to the *ends* of the earth – the margins! – that the risen Jesus sends his witnesses. If, in the Spirit, we can accept the need for our own inner transformations for the coming age, then yes, we are both free and empowered to be witnesses, nothing more – and nothing less.

NOTES

[1] D. Bonhoeffer, "After Ten Years: A Reckoning at New Year 1943", in *Letters and Papers from Prison*, London, SCM Press, 1971, pp.3-17.
[2] See V. Ionita, ed., *Giving an Account of the Hope within Us – the Common Call of the European Churches to Mission*, Geneva, Conference of European Churches, 2001.
[3] The "Charta Oecumenica" in English, French and German is available from the Conference of European Churches, Geneva. The original text is the German. Translations have been made by churches into many other European languages.

[4] S. Barrow and G. Smith, eds, *Christian Mission in Western Society*, London, Churches Together in Britain and Ireland, 2001.

[5] Report available from CEC, Geneva.

[6] N. Sagovsky, *Ecumenism, Christian Origins and the Practice of Communion*, Cambridge, Cambridge UP, 2000.

[7] R. Scott Appleby, *The Ambivalence of the Sacred: Religion, Violence and Reconciliation*, New York & London, Rowman & Littlefield, 2000.

[8] See A. Falconer and J. Liechty, eds, *Reconciling Memories*, Dublin, Columba Press, 1998. See also J. Liechty and C. Clegg, *Moving Beyond Sectarianism: Religion, Conflict and Reconciliation in Northern Ireland*, Dublin, Columba Press, 2001 – a study with profound relevance to many other conflict situations in Europe and elsewhere in the world.

[9] D.B. Forrester, "Christian Political Discourse as Public Confession", in Barrow and Smith, *op. cit.*, p.121.

[10] See report of the Driebergen consultation, *Trafficking in Women in Europe*, Geneva, CEC, 1999.

[11] W. Ustorf, "Farewell to Missionary Innocence", in Barrow and Smith, *op. cit.*, p.144.

[12] N. Boyle, *Who Are We Now? Christian Humanism and the Global Market from Hegel to Heaney*, Edinburgh, T&T Clark, 1999, p.119.

[13] Ustorf, *op. cit.*, p.145.

Called by Name – To Be
More than Ourselves

John 21:15-22: "Simon, Son of John, do you love me?"

Dear sisters and brothers, each of us here has a name. Each name is different, unique to each of us. There is no more beautiful sound, it has often been said, than hearing ourselves called by our name. On Easter morning, as recorded in John's gospel, it is through the calling of a single name by the risen Lord that the news of his resurrection first breaks through: "Mary!" So in this later Easter story also told by John, Jesus – three times – calls his disciple by his full name: Simon, son of John.

Our names are not just "labels". They are more precious than that. They were given to us by those who brought us into the world through their love, and they express something of that love. They tell us something of what was dear to our parents, and about the life and times into which we were born.

My own names are a strange mixture. "Clements" is an English name but very close to the French. My father's family goes back several generations to the Huguenots, those Protestants who fled religious persecution in France in the 17th century. Many of them settled in south-west London, where my father came from. My forenames, or Christian names, came to me somewhat accidentally. "Keith" is a Scottish name, but as far as a I know I have no Scottish ancestry. What happened is that my parents were missionaries in China, and my mother, having already produced two sons, was absolutely certain that her third child would be a girl. So certain was she, that in advance she had chosen girls' names for me, and neither she nor my father had given a thought to any possible boy's name. So when I arrived in the world and informed them that I was in fact a boy, there was something of a crisis. The missionary doctor who attended my mother was a Scotsman, Dr Keith Cameron. So without more ado, my parents decided upon Keith for my first name. But in our family it was also the custom to have a second Christian name. This matter was quickly solved too. The second world war was being

Sermon preached at the opening service of the first meeting of the newly-elected CEC central committee, Morges, Switzerland, 12 November 1997.

fought, and although we were in far-away China my parents were very patriotic Britons and so decided to honour me with the name Winston.

So my name tells a story, as I expect many of yours do as well. They speak of who we are, or at least who our parents wanted us to be. They also of course tell a lot about our nationality, our culture and our history. Even though today there's a lot of movement of people around Europe, you don't expect to find many people called Papaderos in Finland, or Jones in Portugal, or Rusterholz in Holland. And some names convey the particular church tradition into which we have been born and brought up, perhaps even a particular saint of special significance for our family.

"Simon, son of John": an Aramaic name of a Galilean fisherman, son of another Aramaic man and his wife, from the town of Capernaum. Jesus addresses his disciple by name, with all the particular meaning of personality and parentage and culture which that name carries. That is reassuring. It should be especially reassuring to us gathered here from all parts of Europe, from many countries and cultures, languages and confessions. Jesus recognizes, accepts and affirms our particular identities. However experienced we may be in international and ecumenical gatherings, coming to a meeting like this can be a little unnerving. At times we feel like asking, "Can someone be so different from me and still be taken seriously?" Or, even more disturbing, we can find ourselves asking, "If, alongside mine, there are so many different ways of speaking, different ways of living, even different ways of expressing the Christian faith, is mine really as valuable and precious as I thought it was?"

Coming here for the CEC central committee, we bring with us the feelings, the hopes and fears, of a diverse and variegated Europe. We come as representatives of peoples who in many cases are newly conscious of their particular identities, while at the same time knowing that we have to find ways of living together which will be creative and not destructive, as has tragically happened in recent years in some parts of Europe. But the point from which we begin is to hear the word of Jesus, the shepherd who knows his sheep and calls us by name. As the individuals that we are, we are recognized, accepted and affirmed. The particular nationalities, cultures and confessions we bring with us are recognized, accepted and affirmed. Our identities are safe with Jesus.

But that is only the beginning. "Simon, son of John... *do you love me?*" Jesus not only addresses us as the people we are: he calls us, questions us. He wants to know what we are prepared to do with ourselves and with all that we bring with us. Simon, son of John, is an Aramaic-speaking fisherman from Galilee. But he is called to be something more. He is called to be one who feeds the sheep and cares for the lambs in the flock of Christ, and there is to be one flock, one shepherd, including many who are not yet of this particular Palestinian Jewish sheepfold. And so Jesus asks him: "Do you love me?" The first time Jesus asks this question he actually asks, "Do you love me more than these?" What is Jesus referring to by "these"? Some interpreters think that Jesus is asking, "Do you love me more than these other disciples love me?" It could well be that here is a deadly sharp edge to Jesus' question, a devastating recall of how, on the night of his arrest, Simon had indeed boasted that, no matter what the other disciples did, he would lay down his life for Jesus. The rest of the story of that dark night we know, and Simon himself knew too well.

But there might be another, or an additional, meaning to Jesus' question, "Simon, son of John, do you love me more than these?" I can imagine Simon standing there on the lakeside, looking around at the familiar scene: the calm blue waters of Galilee where he had fished for years, the boats drawn up on the shore, the nets drying in the sun and needing mending, the familiar talk of other fishermen and the people coming to buy the night's catch from them; the roofs of Capernaum and Genessaret in the morning sun; and the encircling hills beyond. This was home. Here he had grown up. Here, in this place and in this community, he had learnt so much of what life was about. Here he belonged. And moreover, on this very shore was where he had first met Jesus. How precious, how *sacred*, it all was to him. But Jesus is asking, "Simon, do you love *me* even more than you love all *this*?"

This is the searching question Jesus asks each of us gathered here. Our love for our homelands, our cultures and our confessions, our love for the particular traditions which have nurtured us in life and in the faith, are not denied by Jesus. He assumes them and affirms them. But as the Lord who left heaven and became flesh and laid down his life for us, he asks, "Do you love *me*? Do you love me to the extent of being prepared to leave home and go beyond the familiar, to where I want you to go, and to do what I want you to do, and to become what I want you to be?" It is this question of Jesus that continually challenges and inspires what we call the ecumenical movement. It is the question of whether we allow the call of Jesus to be supreme over all the other claims on our love, and to seek his kingdom which transcends all other human loyalties.

One of Russia's great 19th-century saints was St John of Kronstadt, a priest of the poor and sick in St Petersburg. He wrote: "The church is one and the same with the Lord – his body, of his flesh and of his bones. The church is the living vine, nourished by him and growing in him. Never think of the church apart from the Lord Jesus Christ, from the Father and the Holy Spirit." We are together here in Morges, because we believe that the God and Father of our Lord Jesus Christ wishes his glory to be revealed in and to Europe. It is the glory which was seen in Jesus himself, a very strange glory by the world's standards. It is the glory of love, manifested in the lowliness of service which takes the basin and towel and washes feet like a servant, and is consummated on a cross. It is to be seen in a community motivated by that same love, where the one-ness of Jesus' followers in love will testify that God has indeed sent his Son into the world, that the world might believe.

We are here because we believe that this love is what will reconcile, heal and save Europe and the whole world, and bring new life. In being here together, we are daring to say that we are part of a fellowship which is already experiencing something of this new life; and because we love Christ above all else we are ready to learn new things together, do new things together, take on new adventures of service and witness together, for his love's sake. We are daring to say that we are willing to offer him our names and our identities for the sake of the new and wider commu-nity, reconciled and reconciling, that he is calling into being. Jesus wants Simon, son of John, to wear a new name, carry a new identity: Peter, the rock of the new community, the universal fellowship being created among all peoples.

This is a very demanding and costly love. That is made clear for example in the other circles of stories about Simon Peter, as told by Luke in the Acts of the Apostles. Especially challenging is the story of how Peter, while staying at Joppa by the sea, saw that strange vision of a great sheet coming down from heaven, filled with all kinds of creatures, clean and unclean according to Jewish law, and being told to kill and eat. He responds, "Lord, I have never eaten anything that is profane or unclean." A voice is heard, "What God has made clean, you must not call profane." And no sooner does this happen than the gentiles are knocking at the door below. The mission is widening. New frontiers are being reached. Love for Jesus who loves all without distinction carries the apostle to strange and unfamiliar and sometimes frightening worlds. But love for Jesus also brings its own strength and courage for the journey.

Back to our story by the lakeside. Simon, son of John, having told Jesus three times that he does love him – and now with his special name "Peter" restored to him – is told by Jesus by what death he is to glorify God. Like Jesus, he too will be crucified. But Peter wants to know what will happen to "the other disciple": "Lord, what about him?" Jesus' answer is short and sharp. "What about him? If you really love me, even if he lives till I come again, surely that will not matter to you? Follow me." We have one work to do as sisters and brothers and in the coming years of this central committee. We all share in that one work. In it, we shall have different responsibilities. Some will be elected to particular, prominent positions. Others will not. But what is that to us? All of us matter. We bring ourselves, our names, and all the riches of our particular contexts and traditions, to him. He will make of them what he wills and can use all of them in his purpose of revealing the Father's glory. To each of us, the one and the same question is addressed: "Do you love me?"

Europe Is Meeting

Mark 6:35-37: "When it grew late, his disciples came to Jesus and said, 'This is a deserted place, and the hour is now very late; send them away so that they may go into the surrounding country and villages and buy something for themselves to eat.' But he answered them, 'You give them something to eat.'"

Wales so often produces delightful surprises. A few years ago, one of the bishops of the Church in Wales invited me to come and speak at a meeting for people from all over his diocese on "The Churches and Europe": an unlikely topic, you might think, for folk among the hills of North Wales. After I had spoken, people were invited to tell of their own experiences of Europe. There was no shortage of volunteers. Someone spoke about the link her parish had with a church in Holland. A priest said how valuable it had been to have had part of his theological training on the continent. Others shared how during the cold war they had made friends with people behind the iron curtain. Finally, there marched to the microphone a retired army officer, ramrod-straight back and bristling white moustache. "Oh no," I thought, "now we're going to be reminded why we fought the second world war and how these Europeans need to be kept in their place."

I couldn't have been more wrong. He was a lay-reader, and a few weeks previously he'd gone to take evensong in a little church way up in the hills. When he got out of his car, the churchyard seemed to be a mass of jeans and rucksacks, and he was accosted by a party of young people. They turned out to be Germans from the city of Darmstadt, waiting for the service to start. "So", he said, "we had a bilingual service, English and German: best evensong we've ever had there."

Europe is *meeting*. In Cardiff this weekend the heads of governments in the European Union are gathering. Not suddenly and unexpectedly, but with carefully prepared speeches and with civil servants at their elbows, armed with facts and figures. They are meeting to

Sermon preached at the Norwegian Sailors' Church, Cardiff, Wales, during the EU summit meeting in Cardiff, 14 June 1998, and broadcast on BBC radio.

argue about economics and social legislation. We may find the debates confusing and tedious. But what they eventually agree upon will affect our lives and the lives of millions, not only in the European Union but in Europe as a whole and the wider world too. And if at times their meeting resembles a fight rather than an evensong, let's thank God that here at any rate Europe is fighting around a table rather than on the fields of battle which have brought untold ruin and grief twice this century.

Europe is *meeting*. That's good news, whether the meeting is in a remote Welsh churchyard or at the conference table and in front of the cameras. And both types of meeting are crucial. Some of us here this morning were among over 10,000 Christians from all over Europe, East and West, who in June 1997 year gathered at Graz in Austria. We met to pray, to study and celebrate together the theme of "reconciliation". Reconciliation means the overcoming of enmity and conflict with understanding and friendship, in a new common life of sharing and caring. In fact, it's not easy to speak of reconciliation in Europe today. In Graz, I recall the man who turned up near midnight in the place where I was staying, looking for a bed, having journeyed all the way from the tortured city of Sarajevo. I recall the Albanians who brought with them their heart-rending stories of violence, and the near-chaos to which they would have to return. There were the Russians who were asking whether the old East-West division was really over, or simply being replaced by a new division intended to keep them out of economic progress and security. And from Western Europe there were the people representing the unemployed, the migrant workers and asylum-seekers, wanting to know how we could talk about a "new Europe" when so many people on its streets are excluded from its good things. For that reason, it's good to know that the "unemployment action plan" is high on the agenda at this Cardiff summit.

Europe is *meeting*. Often in a meeting, there comes a decisive moment when we have the opportunity to make something new and better, or when we turn away again in fear or indifference. In our gospel reading, we heard the story of a great meeting when thousands gathered to hear Jesus. At the end of a long day in that remote place the disciples suggest to Jesus that he send the people away to find food for themselves. "*You* give them something to eat," says Jesus. "We can't afford to," they reply, "we have barely enough for ourselves, only five loaves and two fishes." However we explain the miracle that follows, the message is that when in faith we are prepared to meet to the point of sharing what we have, however little it seems, unexpected results can follow.

Sending away, or sharing, is a choice Europe has today. In the grounds of the offices where I work in Geneva stands a monument to former division, now thankfully overcome: a slab of the Berlin wall. But it prompts me to think of Europe as rather like a street where for so long the inhabitants were separated from each other by high walls, and people said, "How awful these walls are!" Now the Berlin wall has gone and other walls are coming down, and people can actually see who their neighbours are – and are so often saying, "How awful these people next door are!" They have said it in the former Yugoslavia where "send the people away" has turned into the horrors of so-called "ethnic cleansing". We are saying it on the borders of Europe as it becomes ever harder for people to find refuge and asylum. And even some Christians are getting close to saying it right across Europe, as the ancient divide in Christendom between the Orthodox East and the Western churches shows signs of reinforcing itself. How good it is that in this service the great hymns of Wales and the glorious chants of the Orthodox church are heard together!

Talking about sharing rather than sending away sounds airy-fairy stuff compared with the hard realities of power and economics to be debated in Cardiff over the next two days. In fact in the long-term, sharing is the only realistic option for Europe as a whole and for Europe's relations with the wider world. The leader of the democratic revolution in Czechoslovakia, Vlacev Havel, has warned that if the West doesn't help the East, the East will destabilize the West. He wasn't making a threat, but simply pointing out that this is how the world is. And if Europe doesn't act justly towards the wider world there will one day be little in the wider world to sustain life in Europe. Again, that's not a recipe for fear. It's simply recognizing realities: that in the world as God has made it, justice and humanity are not extras to day-to-day life but its foundation. If you turn away your neighbours you will one day have no neighbour to care for you. In the long run we cannot have a peaceful world if it's an increasingly unjust or unequal world.

The words of Jesus are the stark truth. But they also give us a wonderful promise, for justice and humanity are themselves the gift of God, the God of grace who is always ready to do the unexpected when we open ourselves to him and to others. What happened in that remote Welsh churchyard can be a parable for all our meetings. In that unexpected encounter, it could have been said, "Sorry, but don't you think it would be better if you went off and had your own service somewhere else?", or "Sorry, but the service is already prepared and we can't alter it now", or "Well, you can come in and sit at the back but it will all be in English"; or, perhaps not said out loud but inwardly, "Actually I don't feel comfortable with Germans; the war and all that." But no, there was openness, real meeting to the point of sharing, and something beautiful and totally unforeseen happened. The grace of God broke through, and everyone went away with more than they'd dreamed of receiving.

Europe is meeting, in all sorts of ways. May that same grace be upon every meeting – even on Cardiff this week.

Begging for Unity

"I therefore, the prisoner of the Lord, beg you to lead a life worthy of the calling to which you have been called..." (Eph. 4:1).

"I... beg you." A very strong word. Paul doesn't just suggest, advise, propose or counsel. He doesn't just ask, request, or even exhort. He *begs*. It's the strongest word he can use to say that he wants members of Christ to bear with each other in mutual love, making every effort to maintain the unity of the Spirit in the bond of peace. Begging is what we do when we're desperate, when we cast all other considerations to the winds, when nothing else matters but what we need and want. Respectability and dignity certainly no longer matter to the beggar.

Some years ago, a solemn young scholar from England went to Glasgow in Scotland for a week, to pursue some research in the archives of the university library. Late in the morning of his final day there, he returned to the apartment where he'd been lodging for the week to collect his belongings before going to the railway station. By agreement with the landlady who had gone away for the day, he let himself in with the borrowed key, sorted out his belongings, deposited the key on the table inside the door, went out, snapped the door shut – and realized that his suitcase was still on the other side of the now locked door. Panic! He had no idea where the landlady was, there was no one else about, the apartment was three floors up, and his train was due to leave in thirty minutes. He did the only thing he could do: tore down the stairs and out into the streets, racing up and down like a madman until at last he saw someone who could help: a window-cleaner loading his ladders onto his truck. Waving his wallet he *begged*: "Can you help? You see that apartment up there, with the window just open? I'll pay whatever you want." A few minutes later, his suitcase was back in his hand, his wallet slightly thinner, and relief all round.

You can imagine how he felt. I certainly can, because that dignified scholar suddenly turned beggar was me. Begging is what the most des-

Sermon preached at the opening eucharist of the council of the Lutheran World Federation, Commugny, Geneva, 11 June 2001.

perate people of all do: people who are starving, people who are homeless, a man with leprosy wanting healing, a synagogue ruler whose
daughter is dying, a Syro-Phoenician woman whose child is possessed.
It's with the same urgency that Paul begs for love, peace, reconciliation,
unity.

Today, it is *we* who are begged to live and practise a life of community, of mutual love, of making good the unity of the Spirit in the bond
of peace. Where is this desperately begging voice coming from?

In the first place, as for Paul, it is coming from the gospel itself. Paul
has spent the first three chapters of his letter painting his vision of the
gospel on a huge canvas and in splendidly glowing colours: the gospel
of God's great and glorious purpose in Jesus Christ, his plan for the fullness of time to gather up all things in him, things in heaven and things
on earth; the gospel of the glorious inheritance among the saints, the
working out of the greatness of God's power when he raised Jesus from
the dead and seated him in the heavenly places, above every name that
is named, not only in this age but in the age to come; the gospel which
is that gentile and Jew, those who were far off and those who were near,
have been reconciled and brought together through the blood of Christ,
into one new humanity in place of the two; it is the gospel that the age-
long mystery of God's purpose has at last been revealed to humankind,
that the boundless riches of Christ are for all people, that we all have
access to the one Father; it is the gospel which prompts the prayer that
we may have power to comprehend with all the saints what is the breadth
and length and height and depth, the love of Christ that surpasses knowledge; it is the gospel which stirs the outburst of praise to a God who can
do far more than all we ask or imagine, to whom be glory in the church
and in Christ Jesus to all generations – Amen!

How magnificent. Perhaps, too magnificent for mere mortals to grasp
or even dare to look at, as Isaiah felt when he beheld the Lord, high and
lofty in the Temple, and all his glory. It is indeed a heavenly vision, but
we are on earth, and of the earth. How do we know this gospel isn't just
a fantasy of dramatic images and high-sounding words?

"I, therefore, the prisoner in the Lord, *beg* you... to live a life which
in human form, here and now, puts into practice what this gospel of reconciliation means. Because if you don't, there's no evidence that we
really believe it, and no reason why anyone in the world should believe
it either." Paul begs desperately for a community of mutual love, peace
and reconciliation because that is the only way of showing the gospel is
real and not a fantasy. Otherwise it's as useful as a suitcase the other side
of a locked door. Not by magical wonder-workings, nor by overpower-
ing intellectual arguments, but by humility, gentleness, the patient weav-

ing together of the frail relationships of peace is the gospel made visible in our world, is the coming-into-being of a new world made credible. It is first of all the gospel itself which begs for a reconciled and reconciling community.

In the second place, this primordial urgency of the gospel begging for reconciliation is for us at the start of the third millennium underscored by our Christian past. There is a great English hymn which runs:

> Thy hand, O God, has guided thy church from age to age.
> The wondrous tale is written full clear on every page.
> Our fathers owned thy goodness, and we their deeds record.
> And this was all their witness: one church, one faith, one Lord!

I love that hymn. But today we can no longer sing it so innocently. The study of church history has proved to make difficulties for Christian propaganda. Not every page has a wondrous tale to tell, not even here in Geneva. In the struggles for Christian truth the truth of love often became a casualty. Some pages have to tell of Christians condemning each other, anathematizing each other, burning each other, drowning each other. The big Lutheran churches of Europe were not always kind to the smaller evangelical communities, which in turn were often judgmental towards their big brothers and sisters. Rulers went to war in the name of religion. We can blame kings and emperors for exploiting religion for their political interests but then we have to ask why Christianity allowed itself to be so easily exploited, becoming part of the political problem instead of the answer. We've always known this, but today we live with an unprecedented awareness of our past. Our history is examined surgically by scholars, not necessarily anti-Christian but not seeing their primary task as being to comfort us with stories of how nice the Christian record is, but rather to show it as often an all-too-human story.

We can neither excuse our history nor forget it. Nor can we pretend it doesn't matter, since we are products of our history and we cannot understand ourselves without knowing of our past. We cannot undo our past of division and conflict, but we can re-examine it. More important still, we can *redeem* it by seeking to discern whether now, today, there are possibilities of reaching reconciliation and unity which could not be seen in the smoke and confusion of the battles long ago. When the agreement on justification was signed in Augsburg two years ago, it was an especially good sign for Europe, still inheriting the effects of the wars of religion, as well as for the worldwide Lutheran family and the Roman Catholic Church.

And if we cannot for the moment redeem it, we can at least pray for its redemption, and pray for that redemption together. All of you, I am sure, will be sad that you cannot meet, as originally hoped, in Bethlehem and Jerusalem. How we pray for the peace of Jerusalem today! I am thankful that I have one blessed image of reconciliation from a visit to Jerusalem. It was a few years ago, when I was invited to join a group of church leaders from Ireland – north and south – to Israel-Palestine. It was especially moving to accompany a party from one divided society on pilgrimage to another wounded part of the world. Those who have been to the Church of the Holy Sepulchre will know that the innermost shrine, according to tradition the tomb where the body of our Lord lay, admits just three people at a time. On our visit there, I was about to follow in with the Anglican Bishop Sam Poyntz, and the Presbyterian minister Gordon Gray, when I felt a tug at my elbow and a voice whispered, "Keith, do you mind if I go in next?" It was the Catholic bishop, Tony Farquhar. I gladly stood by, for I realized what would now happen: Irish Protestant, Catholic and Anglican would pray together, bringing to the most sacred spot in all Christendom the sins of Christendom of which they knew only too well in Ireland; bringing for healing the pain of centuries. The apostolic begging for peace reverberates through the call of the ages at the end of which we stand, or rather should kneel.

In the third place, the apostolic begging for peace and unity, echoed by our past, is amplified a hundredfold by our present world, a world of tragic conflict. It is surely significant that you have chosen as the theme of your next assembly in 2003 "For the Healing of the World", while we in CEC have chosen for our assembly to take place in Norway the same year the theme "Jesus Christ Heals and Reconciles – Our Witness in Europe". Let us be quite frank: however much we in the churches may be occupied by the niceties of our official confessional positions, neither the political decision-makers nor the masses of ordinary people suffering from war, economic exploitation or racial oppression are in the least interested. People are begging for signs that peace is practicable and possible. One of the prophets for Christian unity from my own tradition was J.H. Shakespeare, secretary of the Baptist Union of Great Britain in the early part of the 20th century. In his book *The Churches at the Cross-Roads*, written just after the catastrophe of the 1914-18 war, he tells of one of the impulses which drove him to seek a new vision for the churches:

> How well I remember walking up and down on a calm Sunday evening by the sea-shore with one who had lost two gallant boys, one in France and another beneath the burning Eastern sun. As he told me of the awful struggle raging in his soul, how he had prayed and prayed that they might be spared, and then of the wreckage and midnight of faith when both fell, I saw that in this coming time which will have suffered and lost so much and in which so many lights

have gone out, the sects as such can do nothing at all. The things they stand for in their divisions may be true and good in so far as they go, but they do not matter. They simply and finally do not matter. If the churches can together keep one steady light burning to guide the tempest-tossed to the haven, then in the name of God let them do it.

There speaks a voice, not just in the aftermath of that conflict of our grandparents' time, but from the tragedies also of Rwanda and Congo, from the former Yugoslavia and Sri Lanka and the West Bank and Gaza and from whatever fields of conflict the cry of the bereaved is heard: "We *beg* you, you who name the name of Christ, to live up to your calling as exemplars of peace and reconciliation."

In Europe, we are trying to respond to that contemporary voice. The churches of Europe of all traditions – Roman Catholic, Protestant and Orthodox – now have laid before them, and inviting their adoption, the "Charta Oecumenica: Guidelines for the Growing Cooperation among the Churches in Europe". It invites common commitment by the churches towards proclaiming the gospel in Europe and acting together accordingly; towards accepting our common responsibility in Europe, especially for peace and reconciliation and safeguarding the environment and in relations of dialogue and respect towards other faiths. The commitments are stated very simply – some people will say too simply, even simplistically. But it is always the simple callings which are the most challenging and costly to put into actual practice. I believe the Charta is a way of recalling us to the stark simplicity of the apostle Paul's desperate plea for humility and gentleness, for bearing with one another in love, for maintaining the unity of the Spirit in the bond of peace.

The Charta was launched at the Ecumenical Encounter which took place in Strasbourg just after Easter 2001 – an Easter which was of especial joy since it was celebrated by the Western and Eastern churches on the same day. That Ecumenical Encounter comprised a hundred church leaders from all the confessional families in Europe, and an equal number of younger people. From those younger people we truly heard the contemporary voice. Some observers thought that these younger people were rather quiescent compared with the youth of the 1960s and 1970s. But young people today are not so much interested in revolutionary talk – certainly not those from Central and Eastern Europe who know that a lot of such rhetoric is what betrayed their parents' generation. They are more interested in the far costlier challenge of simple integrity: the need for the church to be in actual life what it should be, a true community of reconciled and reconciling people.

And so it is when we think of the global challenge of our time. In attending the English-speaking Lutheran congregation in Geneva, part of my education into the Lutheran culture has been to appreciate the wording of the baptismal vows, especially when it comes to talking of the devil. Maybe Lutherans (American ones, at any rate!) have some special acquaintance with Satan which have led them to this choice of language, but I am always intrigued by that question: "Do you renounce all the forces of evil, the devil and all his empty promises?" All his *empty promises*. I am sure that during your Council meetings there will be much talk of globalization and its dangers. Here in Europe, many people will do quite well out of the new global market economy – and many people will be hurt by it. But everyone is endangered by its chief threat, which is its *empty promise* of an infinity of choices laid before us as consumers. It is an empty promise because we live in a finite world of limited resources, resources not be grasped by us individualistically but to be shared communally.

In the light of that hard reality, the apostle Paul's words beg us even more insistently through the crisis of our own time. They are a "Charta Oecumenica" for the whole planet, all its peoples and creation itself: humility, gentleness, patience, bearing with one another in love, making every effort to maintain the unity of the Spirit in the bond of peace.

With those words in your ears and in your hearts and your minds, delivered by the apostle, echoing from our corridors of our past and amplified by the cries of our world today, may you enter upon your work. May you be led by the Spirit of peace to know more of what the ministry of reconciliation means for yourselves and for the whole church of God in our time. And in the preceding words of the apostle: "To him who by the power at work within us is able to accomplish far more than we can ask or think, to him be glory in the church and in Christ Jesus to all generations, forever and ever. Amen."

Who Rules – and How?

Ephesians 1:22: "And he has placed all things under his feet."

What an extraordinary claim, a stupendous claim, the apostle makes: God has placed everything under the feet of Jesus, a Jew who had recently died a disgraceful and horrible death by order of the greatest imperial power of the day. This is the affirmation of Ascension day. In a world where everyone assumed that power meant the Roman legions, and authority the diktat of the emperor, the real Lord is declared to be Jesus who died on the cross which the Romans reserved for torturing to death the worst class of criminals. In the world which today assumes that ultimate power is wealth and military muscle and the ability to manipulate public opinion, the real Lord is again declared to be this Jesus. God has placed all things under his feet. This is the affirmation of Ascension day.

All things! The apostle sets no limits here. He speaks of God raising Jesus from the dead and seating him "at his right hand in the heavenly places, far above all rule and authority and power and dominion, and above every name that is named, not only in this age but also in the age to come". All those forces, natural and supernatural, those we imagine and those we can barely conceive of, death itself and whatever lies beyond death – all are ultimately subject to Jesus Christ. This is the affirmation of Ascension day.

This great declaration is not only to be affirmed, but has also to be connected to our present-day lives and to the realities of the world we are living in today. In fact it is not so easy to speak of "the world today" as if it was completely separated from the past. One of the difficulties we face in Europe today is that of having to cope with the continued legacy of our past, and among the forces and powers that we have to contend with are the continuing memories which still dominate much of our outlook and attitudes. We are faced with this, as we gather here in this great

---

Sermon preached for Ascension day eucharist, 21 May 1998, in the Apostelkirche, Münster, Germany, during the first meeting of the CEC commission on churches in dialogue.

historic city of Münster. It is a privilege for those of us who are guests here to share in a small way in the commemoration of that great event, the treaty of Westphalia signed 350 years ago this year in this city. It was indeed a decisive event, marking the end of one of the most terrible periods of conflict that Europe has ever endured. I know that church historians cast doubt on whether Martin Rinckart's great hymn "Now thank we all our God" was actually written to celebrate the peace of Westphalia. But whenever I sing it I imagine myself here in 1648 falling on my knees in gratitude that such a war, with its accompanying scourges of wanton destruction, rape and famine, was over.

Cuius regio, eius religio is the Latin phrase we all associate with the peace of Westphalia. "Whoever is the ruler, his is the religion." That was one of the underlying principles of the treaty. One of the grimmest aspects of the thirty years' war was that, in origin at least, it was a "war of religion". Therefore the most practicable solution was to re-draw the map of Western Europe along lines of religious allegiance. Where the ruler chose to be Protestant, let that territory be Protestant: where he or she chose to be Catholic, likewise. Let us recognize each other's boundaries. That stopped the fighting. But did it in fact bring national sovereignty in a way which was to sow the seeds of further conflict later on, down to our own century? Moreover, did it forge a link between religion and state which left out of account that the church is not first and foremost a national entity, but a universal fellowship, the *una sancta*, the body of Christ?

Cuius regio. Christians should always prick up their ears when they hear talk of a *regio,* a ruler. Earthly rule is indeed within God's providential ordering of this world. But governments are not *the* rulers. They too are under the supreme lordship of Jesus Christ, the ascended heavenly Lord. Christianity in Europe is still struggling to find its true relationship to earthly rule and earthly loyalties, in a way which witnesses to the Christian calling of the higher loyalty to Jesus Christ who is the judge and redeemer of all human life, including the social and political realm. And because our Lord is ascended far above all rule and authority on earth, we belong to a universal fellowship which rises above all national interests and conflicts. I hope that our ecumenical gathering here in Münster, from so many different countries in Europe, is itself an expression of this belief in a universal fellowship under a universal Lord.

Cuius regio? Who is the Lord whom we really obey? In Münster, we are not all that far from Barmen in the Ruhr, where 54 years ago this month, in May 1934, the free synod of the Evangelical Church made its famous declaration which founded the Confessing Church. In face of all the would-be powers of rampant nationalism, racism and militarism seeking to take over the church, its opening words rang out: "Jesus Christ is the one word of God whom we are to hear, to trust and obey in life and in death." We thank God for the witnesses from Germany this century who point us to the Ascension-tide message. They still speak to us and challenge us. And no people need to hear this message more than those of us who have gathered here in ecumenical fellowship, to further the dialogue among the churches of Europe. Today, we may not have European wars of religion in the old way, but we are only too well aware that religion has again been co-opted to further national and ethnic conflicts. Coming from the British Isles, I speak out of our own experience of thirty years war in Northern Ireland, which we hope and pray has now ended. We meet at the end of a millennium which has been the millennium of division in the church of Christ in Europe. We are called together so that the next millennium may be one of healing and reconciliation, for the wounded body of Jesus Christ on earth and for the earth itself.

"Churches in dialogue" is the name of our commission. The very way in which we carry out our dialogue shows whether we really believe in a heavenly Lord, whom God has set over all things. We are not ourselves the Lord. We too are under his feet. So too are our churches, our traditions and confessions and doctrines. He himself is the way, the truth and the life. We are his disciples, not one another's lords. Christian dialogue began to go wrong on the way to Jerusalem, when the disciples began arguing who was the greatest among them, and when James and John asked for reserved seats alongside Jesus in his glory. Jesus said that that was not in his power to grant, and asked them the more immediate question whether they were prepared to share his baptism of obedience and his cup of suffering. He did not deny the hope of glory, but could only offer his own way of utter humility to the Father's will.

I must confess that while English is my mother tongue, I do think Germans have a better word for Ascension – *Himmelfahrt*: heavenward journey. It connects much better with the gospels' picture of Jesus' ministry as a journey – a journey towards the glory of the heavenly places, but where the route lies through the Upper Room, and Gethsemane, and Pilate's interrogation room, and the cross, that horrible death reserved for the worst class of criminals. This means that our belief in the heavenly lordship of Jesus Christ is inseparable from our own calling to humility towards one another. Dialogue means two people speaking. But there is no point to this unless there are two people also listening. When I was teaching in a theological seminary in England, I used to introduce the course in pastoral theology by getting the students to go off in pairs, for each of them in turn to talk for just three minutes to the other about some aspect of their lives – what they most vividly recalled about their childhood, for example. Afterwards we discussed what it was like simply to *listen* to another person for just three minutes. Almost invariably, the students used to say how hard this was. There was always the urge to interrupt and say, "Just like me!" or "My experience was not like that at all!" We are always more anxious to present ourselves, our own experiences, our own tradition, our own priorities, than to learn from the other person. We want to be in charge. We confuse ourselves with the Lord who is the one Word of God to be heard, to be trusted and obeyed in life and in death. We imagine we are already in glory and able to survey the earth from a heavenly perspective, when in fact we are still very much on earth.

To what, or to whom, are we called to be faithful? It is surely to Jesus Christ himself. And the mark of our faithfulness will be whether we have truly entered into the experience and viewpoint of the other: the Catholic listening to the Protestant, and vice versa. The Methodist listening to the Orthodox, and vice versa. The majority church representative listening to the minority representative, and vice versa. At times we would like to place each other under our feet. Our Lord would rather that we placed our ears to each others' mouths. For we, like everything else in heaven and earth, are under his feet, and those feet are marked with nail-prints.

May this Ascensiontide, therefore, fill us with a truly heavenly joy, freeing us from all anxieties about whether our church, or our nation, or our party, or even we ourselves, are coming out on top. May it free us for real partnership, real brotherhood and sisterhood across all human boundaries, and for real dialogue with one another. With Jesus we have nothing to fear, for God has placed all things under his feet.

Unity? Take a Deep Breath

Romans 8:26: "Likewise the Spirit helps us in our weakness."

I confess to a sense of handicap. A good sermon should somehow surprise the congregation. And here I am, someone who works for one of the ecumenical organizations in Geneva, and it's the start of the Week of Prayer for Christian Unity. I imagine you will not expect to be surprised by what I am going to say. You will think afterwards, "Well, he *would* say that, wouldn't he?" If I could, I would really like to speak about unity without you realizing that that was what I was talking about – until afterwards. That puts me in mind of the delightful story which Charles Warr, for many years minister of St Giles' cathedral in Edinburgh, tells in his autobiography. One day he shocked his fellow ministers when he told them that quite often in St Giles', when leading prayers of intercession, he would include prayers for the dead. Not only were his colleagues taken aback by this, they wanted to know how he got away with such a "Catholic" practice in that citadel of Presbyterianism. "Oh," he said, "it's quite simple. I never *tell* them that that's what we're doing. I just do it."

The key passage selected by the churches of France, who have prepared the material for this Week of Prayer, doesn't shout "unity!" at us in every line. In this passage the apostle Paul is speaking about hope: the hope of liberation when the children of God really will be free and possessed of the full glory of God; when all the creation, now as it were groaning with the pains of childbirth, will be liberated from suffering and decay and share in that freedom and glory. In hope, we are saved. In that hope, we can now live. But the question is, how do we connect that glorious hope with the way things are now; the way we are now, the way the world is now, and not least the way the churches are now?

"The Spirit helps us in our weakness." It is not simply that here and now things are bad, or at best so-so, and that one day all will be changed.

Sermon preached at the Scottish church, Geneva, 18 January 1998, during the Week of Prayer for Christian Unity.

That would simply be a vacant dream, not a real hope. Rather, Paul is saying that what we hope for, the glorious liberty of God, is already starting to take hold of us. I don't think it's accidental that so often Paul uses the image of childbirth. As a father, I find it a very powerful image too. What happens at birth? There comes into the light of day this tiny, naked, slippery thing, and there's a breathless silence, as we all wait – and then, please God, comes that first, thin, piercing cry: the first breath has been taken. The new-born baby has taken the first step towards living separately from his or her mother. He is so weak and helpless, yet to his aid comes the surrounding, life-giving air drawn into his lungs. It will be a long time before he can talk, or walk, still less feed himself, and in one sense he'll always need his mother. But, while still so weak, the whole of life with all its possibilities now lies before him: thanks to his breathing in the air. The air: what the Hebrew Bible calls *ruach*, what the Greek Bible calls *pneuma*, the same words they use for "Spirit". It is in taking a deep breath, something we have to do all our days, that our new-born helplessness is connected with our adulthood.

The Spirit, the Holy Breath, the life-giving air of God's own being, helps us in our weakness now, as foretaste of what is promised in all its glory. It doesn't matter that we are weak now, so long as we can take that first deep breath and go on breathing. We are on the way. But let's just think about our human weakness for a moment. There are two senses in which we are weak. The first sense is, I trust, obvious to all of us, if we are honest. Any here who think it does not apply to them are free to leave the service at this point, but please mind your head as you pass through the door. It is the weakness of the wayward heart. It is the weakness summed up in the tedious but necessary word "sin". We have all sinned and fallen short of the glory of God. Our hearts are "curved in" on themselves, as Martin Luther put it. We seek ourselves. Even our best and holiest aspirations are so often tainted with self-interest and vanity. It's not just that already our New Year resolutions look a bit dog-eared. Too often our resolutions themselves manifest a wish to be as God to ourselves, rather than a love of God for God's sake, a love of others for others' sakes.

It's just here that Paul speaks an extraordinary word: "The Spirit helps us in our weakness." I say "extraordinary" because our English word "helps" is, if I may so put it, a very weak translation of the word Paul uses. The word he uses is a rather long Greek word which literally means "to take part with", or "to take hold of along with". Sometimes the Holy Spirit is simply thought of as some kind of irresistible force which comes in and overpowers us – or which burns and blasts away our sins and failings and makes us pure and spotless in one fell swoop.

And if we have no such experience we think we are poor, second-rate believers. But the Spirit takes part with, takes hold along with, our weakness.

This is the gospel. The Pentecost gospel is of a piece with the Christmas gospel we celebrate and sing about in carols:

> He came down to earth from heaven
> Who is God and Lord of all.
> Lo, within a manger lies
> He who built the starry skies.

In Jesus we see a Lord who let go of his equality with the Father, and emptied himself, taking the form of a slave, born in human likeness, humbling himself to death on a cross. A Lord who came to where the wayward, lost sheep was. A Lord who emptied himself to accommodate himself to our weakness that we might be exalted with him. A Lord who became what we are, that we might become what he is.

The Spirit works in no less self-humbling ways. Henry Wheeler Robinson, a Baptist scholar of a previous generation, wrote profoundly of the self-emptying activity of the Holy Spirit, continuing the redemptive work of the self-emptying Christ:

> [I]n spite of our sins, the Holy Spirit does not abandon us. He remains to reinforce the voice of conscience, to awaken the slumbering spark of higher aspiration into a clear flame, to bear with us the shame of our broken vow and frequent fall. In this continued fellowship, there is a deeper humiliation for God the Holy Spirit than ever came to God the Son. For Jesus Christ, the enemies were without, not within, and the body was a holy temple for the indwelling Spirit. But in "Mansoul" there are always traitors within the gate, and God must accept an unholy dwelling for his abiding – till he can transform it into holiness. *This* [self-emptying] of the Spirit is therefore even deeper than the [self-emptying] of the Son, whilst continuing his redemptive work.

Searching words indeed.

In this way, the Spirit helps our weakness. This is not a recipe for resignation. It is a summons to hope. It is in the weakness and brokenness of human life that God wants to be, and will be, until the day of its glory and liberation. It is in a confused, divided and all-too-weak church that we are called to believe the Spirit is nevertheless at work. Humanly speaking, these are not good days to speak of Christian unity. Where the churches are in the public eye, it is often for aiding and abetting conflict, or acquiescing in it, rather than for setting an example of overcoming it: see the streets of Northern Ireland, the shattered villages of former Yugoslavia and the killing fields of Rwanda. The trouble is that the Spirit who takes hold of our weakness is not as often in the public eye as we would wish, just as the air we breath carries out its continual life-giving work unseen deep within the cells of our bodies.

Even in our prayers for peace and unity – indeed perhaps especially there – we may well sometimes feel on the edge of despair and not knowing how to pray as we ought, but we may be sure the Spirit is praying within us with sighs too deep for words. Several times I have visited the Presbyterian Church in Lisburn, Northern Ireland, which has twice been damaged by terrorist bombs aimed at the nearby army barracks. Gordon Gray, the minister, showed me the stained glass window, symbolizing the resurrection, which has twice had to be reconstructed out of fragments of shattered glass. It is a beautiful blaze of colour, but try to imagine what it must be like after every such attack to see all that one has worked to create lying broken and splintered on the ground – to say nothing of the havoc and grief wrought by death and injury. How does anyone pray at a scene like that – except with sighs?

But I believe there is a real connection between the fact that people have gone on praying, and piece by piece putting life back together again afterwards, and the fact that Northern Ireland does seem now to be staggering towards long-term peace. Or I think of what happened when war broke out in Europe in 1914. A.E. Garvie, an English Congregationalist, was horrified not just by the event itself but by the wave of anti-German mass hatred which swept Britain (including many church people). He wondered how he could possibly maintain a Christian spirit in his praying and thinking, and decided that even if he could not pray as he knew he ought, each day as long as the war lasted he would read a page of the New Testament in German. He did so. After the war he was one of those who felt able to join with German church leaders in re-establishing links of friendship. One of the first he found affinity with was Adolf Deissmann – who told Garvie that *he* had been reading a chapter of the Bible in English every day, and for the same reason. Even the most fragile and delicate filaments of thought and prayer can be taken up by the immeasurably strong but equally gentle Spirit, and woven into threads which can eventually become strong cables of unity.

The Spirit helps our weakness. There is a second way in which we are weak. Any who think that this does not apply to them are welcome to try to get home afterwards without having had any assistance from others – without anyone to drive your bus; or in a car that has made itself at your command; or without shoes on your feet fashioned by workers you will never see; without walking on pavements laid by other hands than yours. We have not been created so strong that we can do without each other. Human life is life with others, from the time we are held to our mother's breast to the day when we are finally laid, by others, to rest.

God has deliberately made us weak in this fundamental sense. Even if we were not weak in the sinful sense we would be weak in this sense. Jesus, in our gospel pictures of him, is weak in this way, even as an adult. He does not wish to work alone. He calls disciples to share his work and to be with him. On a hot day by a well he begs a drink from a Samaritan woman. He has to borrow a donkey to ride into Jerusalem. He is overwhelmed by a woman's gift of costly perfume poured over him: no one else has ever cared for me like that, he says. He fears being left alone to face his agony in the Garden of Gethsemane: "Could you not watch with me one hour?", he asks his sleeping disciples. And even one piece of his cross has to be carried for him by Simon of Cyrene.

It is this weakness also which the Spirit "takes part with", "takes hold of along with" to create what is really and truly strong: our community together. Elsewhere in his letters Paul uses the body as a picture of community: in themselves, the ear, the eye, the head or the hand are weak and useless. Only together can they be of use. A little piece of ecumenical history: sixty years ago, in Geneva and elsewhere people were just starting to talk about forming a world council of churches. Plans were being laid, arguments were taking place about its size and organization. But what really concerned some people most of all was, who should be its first general secretary? There was a young Dutchman in Geneva, working for the World Student Christian Federation, W.A. Visser 't Hooft by name. He was clearly a rising star in the ecumenical sky, and strongly tipped for the post. But others were by no means sure, especially in America. He was, for one thing, so young (which was hardly his fault). For another, he was so European – again a Dutchman can hardly be blamed for that – and this was supposed to be a *world* council. And worst of all, apparently, not only was he living in Switzerland, he was an enthusiast for that new fiery Swiss theology being taught by the likes of Karl Barth and Emil Brunner. I recently came across a letter written to one of the doubting Americans by that great pioneer of Christian unity, J.H. Oldham. In his letter, Joe Oldham not only thinks that there is a mistaken view of Visser 't Hooft, he thinks there is a mistaken view of Christian community and its leadership. What he says needs to be said again and again:

> It has not pleased God Almighty to create such persons possessing at the same time an all-round balance. We have got to take them with their human limitations and one-sidedness and seek to supplement them with others possessing complementary gifts. So far from rebelling against this limitation it seems to me to belong to the conception of the Body of Christ that no individual is self-sufficient and that we are all dependent on the gifts and qualities which God has withheld from ourselves and given to others.

A congregation of Christ's people does not consist of believing clones, but of people who precisely in their diversity of gifts and outlooks make up the body. And it is the Spirit which enables this to happen, when we realize we do not have to be like everyone else. We do not have to pretend that we are complete in ourselves. We are set free to rejoice in one another's gifts and not worry about our own limitations or condemn others for theirs. It is what we make up together, or rather what the Spirit makes out of us together, that matters. The Spirit lays hold equally of gifts and limitations, and uses them all. That is true of every single community, and on the wider scale in the Body of Christ.

The Spirit takes hold of our weaknesses and invites us into the wonderful, liberating experience of all being givers and receivers to and from each other. That is true not only within a congregation, within a church, but in the relationship of church to church, confession to confession, tradition to tradition. That is what the search for greater Christian unity is about: not just the dull business of formulating agreements to resolve old unhappy things and doctrinal battles long ago, but actually meeting one another and discovering what more of Christ is to be received from one another's treasury of life and faith and thought and worship. Sometimes that sharing still involves the giving and receiving of pain, but it is sharing none the less.

Recalling the world Faith and Order conference at Santiago de Compostela in Spain in 1992, I can still see now the split-second eye contact between a woman priest of the American Episcopal Church and a bishop of the Greek Orthodox Church. We were in a discussion group, talking about how some things change, and some things can never change, in the church. He deeply felt that she, claiming the validity of women's ordination, was mocking centuries of tradition. Even more passionately she denied this, and pointed to the profundity of her experience of God's calling to ministry. But it was that moment of eye contact I remember, when each seemed to glimpse something precious in the depths of the other's soul, and I thought, "They still disagree, but I don't think either of them will ever be quite the same again." For a moment, the Spirit laid hold of their particularity and opened up a new level of community.

One of the great features of today is the way we are being led to discover more and more that the real strength of the church, the strength of true community, lies in allowing our weakness to be met by other's gifts. We men are slowly learning to give up the pretence of omnicompetence, for the sake of a truer partnership of women and men in the church. The church can be far more effective in its mission and witness than when we assumed dominance. So, too, we Christians in Europe and North America are learning that while indeed we took the gospel to the South and the

East, today it is from the South and the East that so much new Christian vitality and hope is coming.

This came home to me personally at the Second European Ecumenical Assembly in Graz, Austria, in June 1997, with its theme "Reconciliation – Gift of God and Source of New Life". The first day was chaotic as thousands were arriving from all over Europe to register and find out where they were meant to be staying. I unexpectedly bumped into an old friend from South Africa, a black Baptist. After the usual excited hugs, I said, "Ruben, what brings *you* here?" "Well", he said, "I'm now working on Archbishop Tutu's Truth and Reconciliation Commission. I've been invited here to speak on it." I thought of the years of apartheid, of our visits to South Africa and all the other ways we tried to express solidarity with the likes of Ruben engaged in the long struggle. Now, he comes to Europe, with its own conflicts and need of reconciliation, to help show us the way. Pray God Europe will have the humility to go on asking for help.

The Spirit helps us in our weakness: the weakness of our wayward selves, the weakness of our limited human selves. The Spirit is real. The Spirit is here. The Spirit is life-giving, from now until that great day of glorious liberty. Take a deep breath, and hope.

On Being Prayed For

Dear sisters and brothers,

We have just heard the apostle Paul, writing from a prison cell, telling his friends in the church that *"Yes, and I will continue to rejoice, for I know that through your prayers and the help of the Spirit of Jesus Christ this will turn out for my deliverance"* (Phil. 1:18b-19). Here Paul speaks about "your prayers", the "help of the Spirit of Jesus Christ", "my deliverance".

Most of us, I imagine, at one or other point in our Christian lives, or for a lot of our Christian life, wonder about prayer, and especially about praying for others. We ask about whom we should be praying for, what we should be praying for on their behalf, how we should best pray for them. And maybe also, if we are honest, we wonder how, if at all, our prayers work, or if they really make any difference, whether to a friend's personal problems or to violent conflict in the Middle East. Due to a personal circumstance which befell me last year, I have been made to think a lot about prayer, but from the other end. I have been reflecting on the experience of being *prayed for*.

Of course I have always known and appreciated that people have remembered me in their prayers. But this was an especially intense experience, as I lay in a hospital bed and day by day more and more get-well cards got stacked on the bedside cabinet, nearly all of them with the message "You're in my – or our – prayers." Many of those first messages came from people in this Ecumenical Centre, including people who are here at this moment. Then, during the following days of convalescence, came cards and letters and e-mails from much further afield, from Britain and Germany, Sweden and Greece and Russia, North America and South Africa. Some of you will no doubt have had a similar experience at a crisis-point in your life.

It is a strangely exhilarating mixture of comfort and discomfort to know that you are suddenly the focus of such intense loving spiritual

---

Sermon preached at Monday morning worship in the Ecumenical Centre, Geneva, 15 January 2001.

concern, the target of prayer-missiles aimed at you from every quarter. The comfort of course lies in discovering that you evidently do mean so much to others. Even people who don't believe in God admit that. The great painter Pablo Picasso was not a believer, but he was very hurt when one day a cousin of his, a devout Catholic, told Picasso that as he was an atheist he didn't see any point in including him in his prayers. Picasso might not have believed in God, but he believed in love and wanted love, however it was expressed.

But being made intensely aware of others' love can also be slightly discomforting. It was almost embarrassing. I ransacked my store of memories to find a parallel, and eventually unearthed that recollection of early adolescent experience – which again some of you also doubtless recall – of being told on the way home from school or after church: "You know so-and-so? She's really keen on you." And you didn't want anyone to be keen on you – well, not *her* at any rate, and not just now. It was nice to be an object of admiration, but you didn't want a disturbance of your life-programme, the claim of another invading your life which you wanted to be under your own control, and which is what you thought growing up was all about. Similarly, to be prayed for brings home to us that in fact we don't belong to ourselves. We are part of a community in which others do have a claim on us, want something from us, even our very existence and survival. Perhaps embarrassment at being prayed for shows we are still, spiritually, early adolescents.

This is where Paul is so fascinating. "Through your prayers and the help of the Spirit of Jesus Christ this crisis of my imprisonment will turn out for my deliverance" – whether a deliverance of release from captivity, or the deliverance of a triumphal sharing of the cross of Christ into eternal life. He – the great missionary and theologian and founder of churches! – does not present himself as a completely self-sufficient hero of faith, in total command of himself and without need of others. He rejoices in being in fellowship with others, in the fellowship of Christ. So he has no qualms about asking for others' prayers. Time and again in his letters he asks for prayers for himself and his fellow-workers, or rejoices that others are already praying for him. As a person in Christ, he is a person in community, with all the mutuality which that means, the sharing of sufferings and consolation and joy in Christ. From beginning to end, the letter to the Philippians is a celebration of the miracle that through Christ we are given a new life in community. In it, Paul's Greek nouns and verbs are saturated with the prefix *sun* – "with". It's a with-life into which we are baptized, with the Christ who made himself one with us, and who enables us to be one with his risen life in the power of the Holy Spirit, and so one with each other. From the imprisoning illusion of our individualistic self-suffi-ciency we are released into the joyful creativity of life together. We grow up, in Christ.

Praying, and being prayed for, both flows out of and recreates our life in community in the Spirit: which is why it is at the heart of our ecumenical life too. Therefore as churches and Christians on a world-wide level we should also ponder more deeply the significance of being prayed for, as well as praying for other churches and communi-ties. During the German church struggle in the 1930s and 1940s, Diet-rich Bonhoeffer once overheard some of his students making rather flippant remarks on learning that Roman Catholics were including the Confessing Church in their intercessions. He rounded on them sharply, saying that he didn't consider being prayed for by others a trivial matter.

How do we really regard the Ecumenical Prayer Cycle? At this ser-vice we remember the churches of Turkey, Greece and Cyprus. We shall do our best to imagine their situations of being a fragile minority in Turkey, of being a great historic Orthodox church and a minority evan-gelical church in Greece, and of being on a still bitterly divided island in Cyprus. But what happens when it is the turn of our own church and country to be remembered? How do we feel when we realize that Chris-tians in the Pacific are praying for us in Scandinavia, or the churches of Cuba and Guatemala are praying for us in the United States, or the churches of east Asia are praying for us in Africa? Do we really believe we need their love and concern at least as much as they need ours? Or do we still live in the illusion of self-sufficiency?

Perhaps if we tried to imagine how they imagine us, how they view and understand us in their praying, we would be both humbled and lib-erated into a deeper sense of who we are and what we are called to do, and how we do belong together: just as I, an English Baptist, found it moving to picture the Orthodox and Catholic candles burning on my behalf in far places, and so was led to cherish more deeply the diverse ways in which the Holy Spirit sets love alight. Our times of prayer should be times when we not only pray ourselves, but consciously give time to allow the prayers of others for us to find their way into our minds and hearts and bodies.

We will shortly be gathering at our Lord's table, to celebrate the feast of communion, of koinonia with and in our Lord and with one another. We meet in joy, yet also not without pain, knowing that as yet not all who confess Christ as Lord feel able to share at the one table. But the joy and the pain meet one another as hope, the hope that we are nevertheless on the way to that full communion, the mutual indwelling of Jesus and his

Father in the Holy Spirit which they desire us to share and enjoy. Praying for one another is an anticipation of that time. And so with Paul we continue to rejoice, knowing that through our praying and being prayed for, and the help of the Spirit of Jesus Christ, this will turn out for our deliverance. Amen.

Reconciliation Takes Time... and Much Else

Genesis 45:3-15 (the reconciliation of Joseph and his brothers in Egypt).
Matthew 5:23-24: "So when you are offering your gift at the altar, if you
remember that your brother or sister has something against you, leave your
gift therefore before the altar and go; first be reconciled to your brother or
sister, and then come and offer your gift."

Many of us have travelled here by air. In one airport or another, as we
were waiting for our flight to be called, we may have heard that
announcement over the public address system: "For security reasons,
never leave your baggage unattended. Unattended baggage will be
removed and may be destroyed." The word of Jesus which we heard in
the gospel reading is rather different. Jesus says there is a time to drop
what you are carrying and leave it. If you are bringing a gift to the altar
and you suddenly realize that you have something against your brother
or sister, or they have something against you, leave your gift there before
the altar, and go and seek reconciliation with them. However precious
your gift is, there's something even more important: to be reconciled
with those from whom you are estranged.

We meet in Graz, a city of beloved memories to those of us who
attended the Second European Ecumenical Assembly here two years ago
in 1997. We celebrated, explored and shared the meaning of its theme:
"Reconciliation: Gift of God and Source of New Life." Now, at this consultation, we are carrying on the work of Graz.

But we are meeting also in the context of a Europe at war. Thousands
every day are fleeing from terror in Kosovo. Millions of dollars-worth of
missiles and bombs are falling and causing a like amount of destruction.
Dare we still talk of reconciliation? What is the meaning of a "charta
oecumenica" for us now?

The war has affected all our churches in Europe, as they have tried to
respond to it. We are not all of one mind, and reactions to the NATO
intervention differ – as I know full well, since the pile of statements

Meditation given at Graz, Austria, at the opening of an ecumenical consultation on preparation of the "Charta Oecumenica", 30 April 1999.

received in Geneva is growing ever higher on my office floor. The only country where the churches are absolutely at one in their reaction is in Yugoslavia itself.

Two weeks ago three of us from Geneva – staff colleagues from the World Council of Churches and the Lutheran World Federation and I myself – were in Serbia for the weekend. The purpose of our visit was, first, to show our concern for and solidarity with our member churches there and to learn of their situation in the conflict; second, to exchange our perceptions and understandings of the conflict and its causes; and third, to seek to identify any possible lines of action we could undertake together, in meeting the humanitarian crisis and even, however modestly, in contributing to the search for peace. We stood by the bombed bridges of Novi Sad, and the gutted buildings in Belgrade. We saw the sights and heard the sounds of war in the night sky.

But we had not gone just to see at first hand what we can all see on our TV screens. We went to meet with the leadership of the churches, especially the Serbian Orthodox Church, to do what can only be done by personal encounter, by sitting down together, talking and listening face to face. We talked about many things, and above all the conflict in Kosovo itself. Here is where our conversation at times was difficult. We all agreed it was a terrible disaster. But why? And who is immediately responsible for the mass exodus of refugees? It not only was borne in on me that this was at the heart of our visit, but I realized that this kind of conversation is at the heart of all ecumenism, when in the midst of conflict one part of the ecumenical family meets another.

If there is such a thing as "cheap grace", an understanding of Christianity which costs us nothing, there is also the danger of "cheap ecumenism" in the kind of conflict we have at present. It can take two forms. On the one hand, we can hurl criticisms, rather like cruise missiles, from a safe distance at another church whose position is alleged to be inadequate. That costs us nothing. On the other hand, we can go and cosy up to the other church and simply say in effect, "it's OK, we're all good Christians really", which also costs little. Much harder is the encounter in openness and honesty as we wrestle with awkward questions of truth and justice; where we take the risk of challenging and being challenged. That is costly ecumenism. It is painful, and reminds us that at the centre of our ecumenism stands the cross.

This way towards reconciliation, true reconciliation, is hard because it requires truth-telling and truth-learning, which in situations of conflict can be very long and difficult. That is brought out in the story of Joseph and the reconciliation with his brothers. It is one of the most beautiful stories, how Joseph and his brothers finally met with tears and hugs and kisses after their long years of separation. But we only heard the climax of the story. As you know, in the preceding chapter there are those odd episodes of how, after their first visit to seek corn in Egypt, Joseph plays all kinds of tricks on his brothers: keeping one of them behind in prison, hiding a silver cup in one of their sacks of corn and then accusing them of stealing it... and so on. What is actually going on? I think it's quite clear there are two Josephs here. There is the Joseph who is genuinely overjoyed at seeing his family again, and longing to be reunited with his dear father and his youngest brother. But there's also the Joseph who cannot forget what his brothers did to him. Even though it is a long time ago, even though he has had a brilliantly successful career in Egypt, he cannot forget what it was like being dropped in a waterless pit and abandoned, and then being sold off as a slave to foreigners. A past like that does not stay in the past, it keeps coming back and needs redeeming.

The truth of his anguish needs to come out if he is really to forgive, and his brothers must come to know that anguish too. The point can then be reached where the truth of what has been done is faced. Then, too, can be discovered the even deeper truth: what has been done was wrong, wicked, sinful and remains so, but it can be taken up and used by God in his saving purposes. Then can come the tears and hugs and kisses.

That is why reconciliation can take a long time. That is why the precious gift we bring to the altar may have to be left unattended for a long while. That may be so also for the particular gift which is our special tradition in the church. We may have to leave it unattended until we have found reconciliation, and then we can bring it in thanksgiving, with the gifts of all of us. It may be risky leaving it unattended. But then Jesus for our sakes left unattended his glory in order to become the child in the manger and the slave on the cross. But in fact what is precious to us is not really unattended. It will not be removed and destroyed. It is safe with the God who cares for all, who calls us to be one, as the Father and the Son are one, in the unity of the Holy Spirit.

Love Truth and Peace

Zechariah 8:19b: "Therefore, love truth and peace."

Fifty years is a long time, but some of us here, at any rate, can just remember 1949. I was a small boy then. I have to confess that I don't recall the founding of Church and Peace (nor that of NATO, for that matter!) impacting on my infant mind. But something else did. That year for summer holidays my parents took me and my brothers from our home in the north of England to my grandmother's home in London. One evening, the older members of the family started talking about the war which had ended four years earlier: the bombing of London, the houses in that very street which had been destroyed, the nearby buildings that had burned for days, the fear that came every time darkness fell. I went to bed that night rather frightened. A few days later I asked my father a question that had been haunting me: "Daddy, how long does a war last?" I had expected him to say something like "three weeks", which to me at that time seemed long enough for anything. I just could not believe it when he said, "Well, this one lasted about six years." That, I suppose, was one moment when I learnt more of the truth about the world I had been born into.

Five weeks ago, and again just two days ago, I stood in the centre of Belgrade after dark, and watched the anti-aircraft shells winding up into the night sky, and heard the sound of missiles exploding, and by daylight saw bombed bridges and gutted buildings, and palls of smoke from burning oil refineries. In a way I felt just like the small boy again. Could this sort of thing really be happening in the heart of Europe, today? The sort of thing my parents and grandmother talked about, and that the war books and films of my youth had entertained me with? Not to mention the horrendous stories being told by the refugees streaming out of Kosovo. Part of me said this was unreal. Another part of me said, "Yes, this really is what the world is like."

Truth and peace. So often we feel driven to set truth and peace over against each other. How do we face the fact of what the world is like, and

Sermon preached at fiftieth anniversary assembly of Church and Peace, Bienenberg, Switzerland, Pentecost Sunday, 30 May 1999.

still believe in peace as the way the world should be? That is the challenge facing a body like Church and Peace, especially on its fiftieth birthday. It is, I hope, the challenge which all the churches themselves feel faced by, especially the churches of Europe at the present time. Realities versus ideals; grim experiences versus visions; the kingdoms of this world on the one hand and the kingdom of God on the other – it seems we are endlessly caught in this dilemma. We can escape from it, of course, in either of two ways. One way is to take the side of what appears to be reality: the world is a bad place, at most we can make the best of a bad job, choose the lesser of evils, reluctantly go to war if we can find enough reasons to call it "just". Another way is to stay with our ideals, our hopes and our visions of peace in a cosy safe haven of dreams, but evading the hard contact with the world as it is, and blaming the world for not following *us* and so ending up in the mess in which it finds itself.

The Christian church however cannot take either way out if it is to be true to its central tenets of belief. Ours is an *incarnational* faith. The Word became flesh. God's own self became part of the stuff of this world which God's own self created, in order to bring it to true life. As Irenaeus in the 2nd century put it, "He became what we are, in order that we might become what he is." If we are to talk about truths, this truth is the bedrock truth for us as Christians. The poet T.S. Eliot spoke well when he wrote that "human kind cannot bear very much reality". But if the incarnation is for us the fundamental truth, then we should not flinch from facing even the ugliest truths about our world.

"Love truth and peace." We can take it, then, that truth and peace need not be set over against each other. Truth is a precondition for peace. South Africa has been setting us a great example here through its Truth and Reconciliation Commission chaired by Archbishop Tutu. Truth-telling is a part of the peace process. Only if there is truth telling about the past can there be real hope for peace in the future. Only if the wounds and sores are exposed can there be healing, only if the sins are confessed can there be forgiveness and reconciliation. It's easy to say this. Actually to carry it out can be painful and costly – and it takes time.

I was last in South Africa three years ago, attending a theological conference in Cape Town. In the course of the meetings, I got to know two people who were discovering the real depth and cost of facing the truth. One was a young black Lutheran pastor. When he was a boy, his family had been among those ethnically cleansed from the Transvaal and dumped in the so-called homeland of Bophutatswana in unbelievably wretched conditions. The other was a white Afrikaner of about the same age, from the Transvaal, from a very privileged background. He was well on the way towards escaping from his cloistered upbringing within the Dutch Reformed Church. He told me that his eyes were first opened to the reality of what was happening in his country when, as an ordinand hoping to become a minister in the Dutch Reformed Church, he was told that he could not be ordained unless he had first done his military service. So here were two young men, both well educated, both of goodwill, showing that they had a common theological interest through attending this conference. You might expect them to have had instant rapport.

They did not, however. In turn, they each told me about their conversation with the other. How fraught and heated it became on both sides. The black Lutheran had wanted to know, how could any white person not have known what had been happening to his people? Did your parents not know? Did they want to know? On the white Dutch Reformed man's side there was hurt that no explanations, no apologies seemed to suffice. Anger bred frustration in return. But they stuck it out. They left the congress on the way to being friends, yet realizing they each still had a lot to learn about each other, and agreed to meet up in the coming days. Truth telling and truth learning is costly and takes time.

This is why we must hear precisely what our text says: "*love* truth and peace": not just seek them, or work for them, or try to establish them, but actually *love* them. When the Hebrew Bible was translated into Greek, in the version we know as the Septuagint, for "love" the translators used here the Greek word which later became *the* word for "love" in the Christian scriptures: *agape*, the love with that special quality of self-giving for the good of the other. Not the love which simply finds the other attractive or appealing, but the love which is prepared to spend itself whatever the cost for the good of the other. The love which above all is seen in the life and death of Jesus. Love truth and peace in this way; love both of them this way. We can go further. The love of Jesus is a love which totally identifies itself with the other: he bore our infirmities and carried our sicknesses, he was numbered with the transgressors. Or as the apostle Paul put it, he who knew no sin was made to be sin for our sakes (2 Cor. 5:21). *Agape* love is love which fuses itself with the other, and shares what the other is going through. We are to risk becoming truth and peace ourselves, even if it means sitting down and talking with indicted war criminals, as five of us did this week with President Milosevic in Belgrade. There is no way to truth and peace other than by the passionate commitment which "bears all things, believes all things, hopes all things, endures all things" and leads to the cross.

In the summer of 1999, we in Europe find ourselves in a situation of failure. The desperate refugee camps in Albania and Macedonia, the destruction in Serbia, are witnesses to that failure. Efforts to impose will by force and domination, whether by the Milosevic regime or by NATO, have ended in a pit of death and anarchy. The wounds go very deep, and will take many years to heal. But it is not enough for us as Christians and peace activists to point the finger at the world and say, "We told you so. You should have listened to us. You should have followed our way." For what has our way been? What did we expect the world to do when faced with churches which in both East and West all too often exist as national entities and indeed are often nationalistic? And, dare I say it, is it not slightly strange that if we are really lovers of peace there should be so many different peace groups in Europe, Christian or otherwise? Should there not be peace between the peace movements of Europe?

"Love truth and peace." These prophetic words are spoken to a people still living with failure. It is the time just over five centuries before Jesus, when the exiles have returned to Jerusalem from their 70-year captivity in Babylon. They have returned to the beloved city of their parents and grandparents. It still lies in ruins, a bleak testimony to the orgy of destruction which swept over it from Babylon. A slow beginning has been made on rebuilding the walls, and laying the foundation of the temple where Solomon's magnificent edifice once stood. But while physically back in Jerusalem, many of the people are mentally and emotionally still in exile: still regarding themselves as the defeated people, and moreover the guilty people. It is in this setting that Zechariah prophesies.

They are a people who know all too well the contrast between great visions and ideals on the one hand, and cruel realities on the other. They have brought back with them the writings of the great prophets who preached before and during the exile. There is Isaiah's great vision: "Behold, the mountain of the Lord shall be established as the highest of the mountains and shall be raised above the hills, and many peoples shall come and say, 'Come, let us go up to the mountain of the house of the Lord'... He shall judge between the peoples... they shall beat their swords into ploughshares, and their spears into pruning hooks;... nation shall not lift up sword against nation, neither shall they learn war any more." And the people roll up the scroll, and look at Mount Zion which still looks a very modest hump, still covered with weeds and nettles.

Or there's the magnificent sermon by the prophet we call Second Isaiah who preached during the exile about a new exodus, a return across a miraculously transformed desert where every valley would be lifted up and every mountain and hill brought low, and the glory of the Lord would be revealed to all humankind. And the people hear this read, and see the straggling new returnees collapsing tired and disillusioned among the ruins. Or there is that marvellous picture, drawn by Ezekiel, of the life-giving waters gushing out from the new temple, flowing out westward revivifying all creation, even the Dead Sea and the desert. And all there is to see is the muddy trench left by the workmen who have gone home because there is no more pay. And all around, far from there being peace, there are the hostile neighbours who don't want to see a single stone replaced on the city walls. Still time for swords as well as ploughshares.

The truth seems unlovable, the peace unobtainable. Zechariah's significance lies in the way he faces this situation. He believes in what the recent prophets have said about a new age of peace and glory for Jerusalem and the world. But he also knew the hard realities facing the people. And the vision he is given is of a project which is both true to that hope, *and* realizable by the people who are actually there now. That is why in saying "love truth and peace" he is pertinent to our situation also.

Behind Zechariah's words, and the long discourse which they sum up, there are two insights which we can take to heart today. I will call them liturgy and locality.

Liturgy! It sounds an unlikely topic for peace activists! And the study of liturgy even more so. A Roman Catholic bishop shared with me a joke: "What's the difference between a liturgiologist and a terrorist?" Answer: "You can argue with a terrorist." But we should not be too surprised that Zechariah had a liturgical interest – if not a priest himself he came from priestly circles and was very concerned for the rebuilding of the temple. And one of the things we are always in danger of forgetting in the modern West is how important ritual and liturgy are. They are the symbolic means by which we express and reinforce what we feel is really important in life. Anyway, it appears that Zechariah was approached by a group of people who wanted to know whether they should still be keeping the fast of the fifth month every year, a time of mourning and abstinence. Now that was very significant, for the fast of the fifth month was in commemoration of the destruction of the temple and Jerusalem, and had been kept by pious Jews throughout the exile. After their return, some were evidently still keeping it. Zechariah's reply is first of all to ask them a question in return: For whose benefit were you really keeping this fast all these years? For God's, or for your own sake, just as you ate and drank for your own sake? And he reminds them of what the former prophets had said was true obedience to God: "Render true judgments, show kindness and mercy to one another, do not oppress the widow, the orphan, the alien, or the poor, and do not devise evil in your hearts against one another." It was because they had not done these things that disaster had befallen the former generations. So that must be the priority again now.

The fast of the fifth month is to be kept, says Zechariah – kept but transformed. It is to be no longer a commemoration of destruction, but a celebration of the new beginning which God is making with his people. Likewise the fast of the fourth and the seventh and the tenth month too, they shall be "seasons of joy and gladness, and cheerful festivals for the house of Judah; *therefore* love truth and justice." God is doing his new thing: being generous in his provision. He is sowing peace, the rain will fall, the wine will flourish, the ground will yield a rich harvest. The people's part will be to love truth and peace in their dealings with one another.

Liturgy is about how we incarnate in drama and symbol our transformation by grace: the transformation from defeat to victory, from bondage to freedom, from guilt to forgiveness, from conflict to reconciliation, from death to life. Liturgy should give us an anticipation of the end. The Lord's supper, the eucharist, is a foretaste of the great feast when people shall come from east and west, north and south, and sit down together in the kingdom of God. But a liturgy which only gives us a forward glance to the end, without helping us to cope with our present struggles and sicknesses, plays false both to our real condition and the way in which grace works. A true liturgy for peace needs to enable us to express the truth of our present conflicts, the hurt and the anger and the bitter desire for vengeance, as in the Psalms: these have to be brought out into the open and offered to God, who knows how to deal with them all. Zechariah does not disparage the keeping of the fast as such. It was good and healthy that mourning was observed for the destroyed temple and the city all those years of exile. There is a time for mourning. Precisely because it has been gone through, there can now be a time for celebration: *Therefore* love truth and peace. To work on liturgies for truth and peace is a task for the churches today.

But now, locality. It is a beautiful and very human picture which Zechariah paints of the new Jerusalem: a city where the streets are full of old people sitting with their walking-sticks, and children playing. A community of shared abundance and security, where people speak the truth to one another in their court-cases at the city gate, and reach judgments that make for peace. It is very practical and down-to-earth. But we might think, isn't this a rather narrow and parochial picture? What has happened to that great prophetic, universal vision of peace over all the earth, of the wolf lying down with the lamb, of the earth being filled with the knowledge of the Lord as the waters cover the sea? In fact, Zechariah has kept that vision. All he has done is glimpsed a way it can begin to be realized. Jerusalem, he is saying, while only one place on the earth, can be such a marvel that people from every other nation will want to come and see it for themselves and worship God there. Jerusalem becomes a particular place with a universal significance. In this way, Zechariah brings together the grand vision and the reality of the world. He doesn't have a grand strategy to impose on the entire world. He has a picture of his own community, which can then attract the rest of the world. A light to lighten the gentiles.

One of the most inspiring places I have ever visited, towards the end of Lebanon's tragic civil war, was the community of Chouifat in Beirut. A big apartment block, it stood right on the so-called green line between the eastern and western sectors of that bitterly divided city. The people refused either to flee from the shelling and the rockets, or to allow their building to be taken over as fortifications by either side. They said, "You are not going to move us, you are not going to divide us, we are staying together." And they stayed. With the help of the Middle East Council of Churches they got a new water supply, they maintained a clinic, they developed their own income-generating industries; they ensured that space was kept open for a children's play ground, free of both rubbish and landmines. That for me is a parable for our times.

"Love truth and peace." Today, we feel strongly the need to try to apply these words on the global level. And indeed we have many tasks to do at the global and international level, and many questions to ask in relation to the Kosovo crisis: about the role of the United Nations, about the real intentions of NATO, about the role of the weapons industry, about the whole global economic order. But might it not be also that now is the time to attend, much more closely than we have ever done before, to the practice of truth and peace at the local level? It is one thing to say how ethnic differences have been exploited by unscrupulous politicians. But why were local communities so susceptible to such exploitation? Are not the real questions about peace for the future, about how local communities can be so empowered and enabled to stand up to and resist those who would divide them and exploit them in their abuse of power? How can we enable and empower local communities to stay together, to become economically and culturally resistant to outside manipulation and exploitation? From Kosovo to Northern Ireland? From Rwanda to Sri Lanka? It is in the love of truth and peace in the local community that universal vision engages with contemporary reality.

Truth and peace do belong together, when they are really loved, loved with the passion of the Spirit, God's own love. If it was T.S. Eliot who said that humankind cannot bear very much reality, it was also T.S.

Eliot who in the same cycle of poems gives us the picture of the transforming love of Pentecost:

> The dove descending breaks the air
> With flame of incandescent terror
> Of which the tongues declare
> The one discharge from sin and error.
> The only hope, or else despair
> Lies in the choice of pyre or pyre –
> To be redeemed from fire by fire.

Therefore, *love* truth and peace.

Healing the Wound:
A Return to China with Bonhoeffer

One of the most satisfying moments in life is when we start to see connections between different and at first sight contrasting elements in our thinking and experience. "Healing" and "reconciliation" can apply as much to the inner personal life as to the outer public world of relationships between peoples, nations and churches. Moreover, the most profound experiences of such healing and reconciliation occur when they embrace both the inner and outer spheres together. In one particular way this became true for me in the last ten years or so. For much of my adult life a good deal of my theological interest has centred on the life and thought of Dietrich Bonhoeffer, and his continuing significance for the shape of Christianity in the contemporary world. Such an interest has never for me been a purely academic affair, but neither for a long time did I think it had much to do with the circumstances of my own birth and upbringing – nor did I think that it needed to have such a connection.

But certain events and travels in which I got caught up in the 1990s altered this, together with the discovery that another active member of the International Bonhoeffer Society, Burton Nelson of Chicago, had like me been born of missionary parents in China. One thing led to another. The result has been, for me, a simple but profound and rewarding education into what "healing the wound" can involve, even in inter-Christian relations, at the international level. The intertwining of grace with the ambiguities of human history calls for a patience, a waiting in humility, which does not sit well with the urge for instant solutions.

The China missionary endeavour: a retrievable past?

For a hundred years, from the mid-19th to the mid-20th century, China was the scene of the greatest-ever missionary exertion by Western Christianity. My parents were part of this enterprise, serving in the China Inland Mission, the Protestant agency that was founded by the redoubtable Hudson Taylor in 1865 and became the largest mission in the whole world. My mother went to China from Australia, where her family had emigrated from England just after the first world war. My father went out to China from London in 1931. They met and married in

Chungking, and served their first term together in Itchang in charge of a transit point for missionaries journeying up and down the Yangtze River. After furlough they made their way back to Chungking in 1938, circumnavigating the difficulties caused by the Japanese invasion of eastern China, and were dispatched on a perilous journey by river and on foot to Gulin, a small, remote town set amidst the mountains of southern Sichuan. There I was born, their third son, in May 1943 (I have always slightly regretted that Bonhoeffer, who had then been imprisoned for about a month, does not seem to have written a letter on the actual day of my birth!). In late 1944, on medical advice relating to one of my brothers, and much against their inclination, my parents decided to leave China. We had an adventurous journey into India and thence back to England. For a long time my parents hoped that this would be a temporary exit. In fact, it was for good.

So I was very small when we left China. My earliest clear memories are of life back in England. But I always have the impression of remembering China. I was continually told stories of life in Gulin: about the colourful characters in the town and in the small congregation my parents established; about the people who came from miles around when they started a simple medical dispensary; about Lao-Ben-Yang, the cook who was a member of the household and who looked after me much of the time (learned from her, no doubt, my first spoken words were in Chinese). Fuh-In-Wan, a place up in the hills which was a centre for mission among the Miao tribespeople, seemed to me a source of stories as remarkable as any in the *Arabian Nights,* as I heard of the breathtaking mountain landscape, encounters with brigands, and devastating thunderstorms. I was brought up knowing China as a place of almost magical beauty and adventure.

But I learned of it too, eventually, as a place of the past. There could be no return. By the time my brother's health problems had been resolved, it was too late to go back. Mao Tse-tung's Long March and the revolution of 1949 saw to that. From being the scene of the greatest Western missionary inflow, Protestant and Catholic, China almost overnight saw the greatest missionary exodus in history. I suppose I grew up simply accepting this. After all, life was here and now in England; cricket and soccer, comics and films. Teenage loves and school examinations were enough to occupy the adolescent soul. But to have been born in China always gave one a kind of pride. None of my peers had had that privilege. When Alan Burgess's book *The Small Woman* made famous the English missionary Gladys Aylward, and Ingrid Bergman in her starring role in the film *The Inn of the Sixth Happiness* made her more famous still, some of the kudos seemed to wash over oneself.

Later historical awareness brought problems, however. One learned about the Western imperialist and commercial inroads into 19th-century China, of the opium wars and the treaty of Nanking, and of the ways in which the massive missionary enterprise had largely followed, benefited from, and often been protected by the gunboat. Still later, to the student of missionary history came the revelation that in the first half of this century many Chinese Christians themselves were resentful at the paternalism of the Western missionary presence, which they felt to be obstructive of the growth of a genuinely Chinese and united church. The missionary exodus that followed the Great Revolution was by no means wholly an expulsion by the wicked communists. In many cases the departure was encouraged by the Chinese Christians, who viewed a continuing Western presence as a hindrance to their witness in the new situation. One had been told that, following the revolution, the patriotic "Three-Self" movement (for a self-supporting, self-governing, and self-propagating church) was simply a front for the communist-dominated church, while the "true church" was underground. Now, it appeared, it was not so simple as that. The concept of a "three-self" church had been born much earlier, in the thinking of no less a person than the pioneer Burma missionary Adoniram Judson. Few people of the missionary generation were prepared to admit the question marks over the story of Western missions in China, a notable exception being David Paton in his angry book *Christian Missions and the Judgment of God*.[1]

All this now added up to a formidable difficulty in owning my past and my inheritance. Had I been born out of a hugely mistaken enterprise? I suppose that my problem was but one tiny, personal focusing of the whole problem of being a Westerner in the late 20th century, faced with the guilt of generations of exploitation of Africa, Asia and Latin America. Did I now have a past, a tradition, that I could own with any sense of respect and gratitude?

Bonhoeffer and the past

Maybe this was why, perhaps subconsciously, in my reading of Dietrich Bonhoeffer during the late 1970s and 1980s I was drawn again and again to his emphasis on the value and importance of consciously standing in a tradition. For Bonhoeffer, one vital ingredient in a fully human existence is an awareness of a historical legacy for which one can be grateful, and which supplies the theme to be taken up into one's responsibility for the future. Bonhoeffer's lifelong love for his own family tradition and for much in his German cultural legacy is well known.[2] It became especially important to him during the uncertainties of war and the perils of involvement in the resistance. On a train journey in 1942 he writes to Eberhard Bethge's younger brother:

> While I'm going through ancient cities and the summer countryside in the glorious sunshine, I keep thinking of you... I have a life which is hardly like yours at all, and which must be strange to you. And yet it is in this long journey, looking at the cathedrals of Naumberg, Bamberg, Nuremberg, at the cultivated fields which are sometimes so poor, and the thought that all this has been work and joy for many, many generations, that gives me confidence that here there is still common ground, a common task, a common hope, something which overcomes the gap between the generations. When one thinks of that, one's own short personal life becomes relatively unimportant; one begins to think in terms of greater periods and tasks.[3]

From prison in May 1944, in the famous "baptismal sermon" to Eberhard and Renate Bethge's son, he writes, "To be deeply rooted in the soil of the past makes life harder, but it also makes it richer and more vigorous. There are in human life certain fundamental truths to which people will always return sooner or later."[4] Indeed, it was the prison experience which, as Ruth Zerner and others have shown,[5] gave a special psychological urgency to Bonhoeffer's "retrieval" of his own past, seen particularly in his attempts at writing fiction and poetry. It was not, however, only his immediate, familial past with which he wished to reassociate himself, but also the great intellectual tradition of Germany as witnessed to, for example, by Harnack's *History of the Prussian Academy.* To Eberhard Bethge he writes disparagingly of the current tendency to return romantically to the 18th century and earlier (not to mention the supposed Teutonic Age glorified beyond belief by Nazi mythology) at the expense of the 19th: "Who bothers at all now about the work and achievements of our grandfathers, and how much of what they knew have we already forgotten? I believe that people will one day be quite amazed at what was achieved in that period, which is now so disregarded and so little known."[6]

The sense of time was central to Bonhoeffer, and therewith nothing was more perilous to responsible human existence than *forgetting.* It is a theme that emerges powerfully in his *Ethics,* above all in his depiction of the "void" that he saw in the contemporary European mind:

> In the face of the peril of the void there is no longer any meaning in the question of the historical inheritance which requires of those who receive it that they shall both develop it in the present and hand it on to the future. There is no future and there is no past. There is only the moment which has been rescued from the void, and the desire to snatch from the void the next moment as well. Already what belongs to yesterday is consigned to oblivion, and the affairs of tomorrow are still too far off to impose any obligation today. The

burden of yesterday is shaken off by glorifying the misty past, and tomorrow's task is evaded by speaking rather of the coming millennium. Nothing makes a permanent impression and nothing imposes a lasting obligation. A sign of the deep forgetfulness of the present time is the film which is erased from the memory as soon as it is over.[7]

To be fully human, therefore, includes the sense of a past that can be retrieved and owned in gratitude and worked upon for the sake of the coming generation.

Return to China

If what Bonhoeffer said was true – and I could not help suspecting that it was – how could I deal with the fact that, not only by circumstances but also ethically, I felt excised from a vital part of my past? "Forgetting" was impossible, and endless efforts at rationalization or self-justification were proving futile. The facts were all too real. The answer came another way, not long after both my parents had died. It was not my own answer, but an answer given to me by others, by the only people who were in a position to offer it.

In May 1994 I returned to China as a member of a British ecumenical study team. As it happened, a good deal of our time was to be spent in Sichuan. From Hong Kong we flew to Chungking. I visited the old site of the mission house where my parents had met and the church where they had been married. The day of our arrival was in fact my birthday, which provided the local representatives of the China Christian Council with a pretext for adding even more festivity to the warmth of their welcome. The real excitement, however, came with the prospect of actually getting to Gulin itself. It was not until almost leaving Hong Kong that we had learned that our party had been granted special permission to journey to Gulin, that area having been strictly out of bounds to foreigners. As it happened, we were the first Westerners to be seen there for forty years.

I need not recount my feelings on the two-day road journey, which had taken my parents many days by junk and on foot in 1938, as the scenery of mountain and river progressively unfolded, just as my father had described it in his unpublished memoirs. Gulin was still essentially as he had portrayed it, and as I too had pictured it from those early childhood stories and possibly (who knows?) my own vaguest memories: grey roofs of cylindrical tiles, crowded streets, the river slowly swishing through. Only a small community of Christians remained, but they included one very old man who could just recall our family, and the welcome was in every way a homecoming. We were taken to the place where my parents had lived, where their chapel and medical dispensary had stood – now much changed but the basic architecture still fitting their description and where I had been born on a stifling night amid smoky oil-lamps and mosquitoes. On our return to the hotel, we found two other Christians waiting for us. Peasant farmers, tired and poorly clad, they had heard of our imminent visit and had walked thirty miles over the hills to meet us. Clearly, something remarkable was happening. That night for our evening prayers I decided that nothing was more fitting than to read T.S. Eliot:

> We shall not cease from exploration
> And the end of all our exploring
> Will be to arrive where we started
> And know the place for the first time.

But all this was as nothing compared to the next day, when we journeyed along deeply rutted roads up into the hills to Fuh-In-Wan. We had to leave our bus and walk the last mile or two down the steep, narrow path. As we approached, we heard the sound of singing. Soon we saw them: nearly two hundred Miao people who had been waiting twenty-four hours for our arrival and had prepared a feast for us. The old chapel had been commandeered by the authorities as a school, but the people still clearly regarded it as theirs. Even the local officials sent to mind us seemed to be touched, as well as highly nervous of what was going on.

We were welcome. I was welcomed back like a long-lost son. We were taken to a simple graveyard and shown the grave of the young daughter of two of my parents' older colleagues: "The loneliest grave in all the world," said one of our party. After the hours of feasting came the most emotional farewell I have ever experienced, amid the chorus, "God be with you till we meet again", sung in Miao. On the long, hot trek back up to the bus, I tried to reflect on what it all meant. Yes, for all the questions about the old missionary endeavour, it was now being remembered with gratitude. It had been deeply costly in personal terms. While still in Gulin the previous night, it had begun to dawn upon me just what it must have meant to my parents: the hazardous journeyings, the sheer poverty and disease, the isolation and loneliness (they only heard of the Normandy invasion two weeks after the event). Edmond Tang, my Hong Kong Chinese colleague, said we had experienced a retrieval of the missionary history.

A few days later in Nanjing, the head of the China Christian Council, Bishop Ting, summed it all up in saying that Chinese Christians were now in a position to offer thanks to the Western churches for bringing the gospel. They still believed in a self-reliant Chinese church, but on that basis were now looking forward to a new *partnership* with their Western sisters and brothers.

We had experienced *grace* at Gulin and Fuh-In-Wan. My past had been offered back to me as a gift; and only as a gift from those people, representative of all the suffering of China, could I have retrieved it. And it had to come at the right time, the "now" to which Bishop Ting referred. Time alone does not heal, but the healing processes need time.

The healing of the wound

In his *Ethics,* under the heading "Justification and the Healing of the Wound", Dietrich Bonhoeffer writes with both insight and restraint of the mystery of the overcoming of guilt in the life of the individual Christian, of the church, and of the world of nations.[8] A complete breach with the guilty past takes place through the church's confession of guilt and the church's taking the form of the cross. For the nations the process is more indirect, "there is only a healing of the wound, a cicatrization of guilt, in the return to order, to justice, to peace, and to granting of free passage to the church's proclamation of Jesus Christ". Bonhoeffer writes realistically that the wheel of history cannot be turned back: "Not all the wounds inflicted can be healed, but what matters is that there shall be no further wounds."

In the history of the Western interaction with China, it is not in fact quite so simple to separate the churches from (to reapply Bonhoeffer's words to this case) the "imperialistic conquest" which was "pursued amid contempt for law and justice and brutal mishandling of the weak". The Western churches have had to wait for their own realization of their need for confession, and for the time when their Chinese sisters and brothers felt able to accept and welcome them again. In this welcome, at the right time, comes the freedom to acknowledge also what was actually good and Christ-like in that former history: the selfless love that did motivate many missionaries, mine and Burton Nelson's parents among them, and which can *now* be disentangled from the darker side of the Western enterprise precisely because that darker side is honestly admitted. The fact that the positive thread in the history is now affirmed by our Chinese sisters and brothers, not just snatched at desperately by ourselves, gives us the grace to own it too.

Therefore I do now have an inheritance with which I can identify, and which I can cherish as of continuing value for contemporary responsibility and the future. Actually, going back to China, pondering that experience, and rereading my parents' accounts of their China days in the light of it have opened my eyes to something I had not quite seen before. Why did they wish to return to China after the war? The religiously correct missionary answer would of course be, "Because they wanted to preach the gospel." I think the real reason was more basic. They had simply fallen in love with China, even with poor, remote little Gulin, and would have much preferred to live there. In his memoirs my father recalls how once in Gulin one of their Chinese friends, having referred to someone from a neighbouring province as a "foreigner", and my father having asked, "Then what does that make us?" replied, "*You* are not a foreigner; you are one of us." That is the tradition that I am glad to have retrieved, a story of how, through friendship, strangers can learn to identify with and even reincarnate something of themselves in other cultures. That is both a gift from my past and a hope for my world.

So I am deeply grateful to have been able to experience not only the retrieval of my own past, but the beginnings of a new relationship between the Chinese churches and the ecumenical fellowship; between, on the one hand, the generation of Burton's and my parents and, on the other hand, the new, rising, and rapidly increasing generation of Chinese Christians who are making room for themselves regardless of what the state does; between the land of our birth and the West. Let the last word be Bonhoeffer's:

> The "justification and renewal" of the West, therefore, will come only when justice, order and peace are in one way or another restored, when past guilt is thereby "forgiven", when it is no longer imagined that what has been done can be undone by means of punitive measures and reprisals, and when the Church of Jesus Christ, as the fountain-head of all forgiveness, justification and renewal, is given room to do her work among the nations.[9]

NOTES

[1] David Paton, *Christian Missions and the Judgment of God* (London: SCM Press, 1953).
[2] Cf. Keith Clements, *A Patriotism for Today: Love of Country in Dialogue with the Witness of Dietrich Bonhoeffer* (London: Collins, 1986), *chap . 5*, "Accepting a Heritage."
[3] Dietrich Bonhoeffer, *True Patriotism: Letters, Lectures and Notes 1939-45*, London, Collins, 1973, p. 136.
[4] *Ibid.*, 295.
[5] In Dietrich Bonhoeffer, *Fiction from Prison: Gathering Up the Past*, ed. R. and E. Bethge with C. Green (Philadelphia: Fortress Press, 1981).
[6] Dietrich Bonhoeffer, *Letters and Papers from Prison*, London, SCM Press, 1971, p. 227.
[7] Dietrich Bonhoeffer, *Ethics*, London, SCM Press, 1971, pp. 85f.
[8] *Ibid.*, pp. 95-97.
[9] *Ibid.*, p. 97.

Afraid of Death – or Life?

Matthew 16:28: "Truly I tell you, there are some standing here who will not taste death before they see the Son of Man coming in his kingdom."

I wonder how you felt as you heard this morning's gospel reading. Of course it is one of the most dramatic episodes in the story of Jesus. Following Simon Peter's great confession of Jesus as Son of God, we now hear Jesus declaring how he must suffer and die and rise again. And we hear how Peter who the moment before had made that great confession now speaks on behalf of Satan himself and says, "Lord, this must never happen to you." We hear how Jesus rebukes Peter, and issues his challenge: whoever wants to be his disciple must deny him- or herself, take up the cross and follow.

Very dramatic, but to many of us also very well-known. As a child in Sunday school I had to learn part of this passage by heart. So perhaps as we heard these words we felt the challenge – *and* sensed a great familiarity. With each verse, we knew what was coming next. Indeed, perhaps you also felt you knew what *sermon* would be coming next, especially on a day when so many people taking part in the ecumenical movement are here. Don't worry about admitting that – I felt the same when I started pondering the passage a few days ago. I almost felt the sermon was writing itself: "... Following Jesus means denying ourselves and bearing the cross... that must be true of the church as a whole and especially the ecumenical movement today... The World Council of Churches must take the way of suffering and self-denial for the sake of the world. Only if they give themselves up will they find their true life..." And so on.

It all may be true. But the very ease with which we have come to say such things begins to trouble me. When we feel so very much at home with Bible passages, and when sermons start to write themselves, we should ask whether we are missing something. It's not enough to expound the teaching of Jesus in a way which simply sounds heroic and makes us feel vaguely excited.

Sermon preached at the English-speaking Lutheran church, Geneva, during the meetings of the WCC central committee, 29 August 1999.

I am moved to say this even more when I contemplate one of the 20th-century Christian figures who has highlighted these words of Jesus so starkly. Dietrich Bonhoeffer died on a Nazi gallows just before the war ended, a faithful witness to Jesus Christ, a martyr for truth and justice. That makes what he himself wrote about the sayings of Jesus on taking the cross so authentic and poignant. His book on discipleship, *Nachfolge*, which he published in 1937 and which we know in English as *The Cost of Discipleship*, is really one long exposition of Jesus' call to follow him exclusively, to bear the cross with him, and at its heart are the words in today's gospel reading. "The cross is laid on every Christian," writes Bonhoeffer, "... As we embark upon discipleship we surrender ourselves to Christ in union with his death – we give over our lives to death... When Christ calls anyone, he bids them come and die." Never has the heart of discipleship been expressed so profoundly and starkly.

Yet, seven years later, while in prison, and knowing just what bearing the cross really meant, even Bonhoeffer himself was taking another look at this theme. I am just one of the many people who have had the privilege of meeting and talking with Bonhoeffer's friend and biographer Eberhard Bethge, the one to whom Bonhoeffer wrote most of his letters from prison. And once I asked if I could see the original of what to me has always been the most remarkable of those letters, the one he wrote on 21 July 1944, the day after the plot against Hitler was attempted and failed, and Bonhoeffer knew that humanly speaking his own fate was sealed. But it is a letter full of gratitude and hope: not a hope that God would get him out of his grim situation, but the truly faithful hope that God will unite us with himself and recreate us as the persons he wants us to be when we live with him completely in this world come what may. That is faith. But he also says that this is quite different from trying to live "a holy life", and that he can now see the dangers of what he wrote in *The Cost of Discipleship* – "though I still stand by what I wrote". You see – and of course I have to say it in this particular church – he was too good a Lutheran to believe that anything we do, however heroic – even bearing the cross – can *earn* God's grace.

If even Bonhoeffer felt we should be careful how we read the call to costly discipleship, we ourselves should take another look at this so-familiar passage and see whether our easy sermonizing about taking the cross is missing something. But how do we enable an over-familiar passage to appear new to us? I once heard a geologist say how, as a student, on field trips he had been taught by his professor to see features of the landscape and terrain he might otherwise miss. It was very simple: "Look at the scenery upside down by bending down and looking at it through your legs." It then looks surprisingly different from the familiar normal view. We can do something similar with this gospel passage – look at it not perhaps upside down but at any rate back to front. Start at the end, and work back to the beginning.

"Truly I tell you, there are some standing here who will not taste death before they see the Son of Man coming in his kingdom" (v.28). An enigmatic saying, but whatever else it is, it's the promise of the coming of God's reign of power and glory which puts death in its place. What Jesus affirms is the fullness of life which God's reign brings: it's coming, and we are called to be more prepared for it than even our own deaths.

Next stage back: "For the Son of Man is to come with his angels in the glory of the Father, and then he will repay everyone for what has been done" (v.27). A message of judgment: but it is still a message of hope, for it will be the establishment of justice, the overcoming of wrong with right.

Back further: the saying about taking up the cross, and losing one's life to find true life (vv.24-26). Yes, it's about dying, but dying not as an end in itself but for the sake of true life and the way to that life.

So right to the beginning of the passage, the saying that Peter finds too hard to take: Jesus must go to Jerusalem and undergo great suffering at the hands of the elders and chief priests and scribes, *and on the third day be raised* (v.21). Jesus foretells not only his passion, but his resurrection too! Our usual reading assumes that Jesus' talk about his suffering and death blots out from Peter's mind what he says about being raised to life. But dare we think that perhaps Peter was also scared of talk of resurrection? If that seems a strange idea, remember some of the accounts of Easter morning, when the first message to those who came looking for the body of Jesus and could not find it was, "Do not be afraid!" The disciples shrank from the cross; they *fled* from the empty tomb. There is a fear of death; there's an even greater fear of life, new life.

This passage, then, is as much about life as about death, about resurrection as much as the cross. It is Jesus offering us God's priceless gift of life, and his challenge is that of asking us whether we want that life so much that we are prepared to let ourselves as we are now be lost for his sake. It is not about taking up the cross as an heroic ideal in itself. It is about embracing God's gift of life, and the cross as the price of that life. The Letter to the Hebrews describes Jesus himself, the pioneer and perfecter of our faith, as the one "who for the sake of the joy set before him endured the cross, disregarding its shame, and has taken his seat at the right hand of the throne of God" (Heb. 12:2). We celebrate the victory of life.

Jesus calls us to take up the cross, but first he calls us to leave self behind, and totally abandon ourselves to let God make us what he wants us to be in God's own life. If we don't do that first, then even the way of the cross becomes co-opted into our self-centred desires and ambitions. It's not always the case that people try to avoid suffering. It can be sought as a cop-out from living a fuller life. Or we can sometimes try to wear it as way of advertising how good and pious we are, or as a way of feeding our self-pity. We can adopt the role of perpetual victim in the drama of life.

Every Christmas, as I expect you do, in our home we get the annual Christmas letters from friends we have collected over the years (they also get ours!). The letters come in varying modes. Some take the form of the Great Annual Success Story: the marvellous new home, the unforgettable summer holiday in some unbelievably exotic place, the progress of the children who are obviously budding Mozarts or Einsteins. Others are more humdrum: "Still here, one more grandchild, been painting the garage, only two more years to retirement."

But there's one friend of nearly thirty years' standing, whom I shall call Robert though that's not his real name, whose letter we opened each Christmas with some trepidation. It was always a catalogue of woes. He is a minister in England (I won't tell you which denomination) who has worked in various posts and chaplaincies and ecumenical projects, and in the course of time his letters more and more became lists of the people he'd fallen out with, the congregations who didn't want him any longer as pastor, the bishop who told him that his ecumenical work in that part of England was a disaster... and so on, and always ending up with a diatribe against the reactionary and spiritually blind state of the churches in Britain. It eventually dawned on us that Robert in a peculiar way actually enjoyed being the victim and martyr, the prophet who was always being stoned. That was sad, because it meant that he was not able to share and use the real gifts he had, and take responsibility for finding a way of really influencing the ways of the church for good.

That, I am glad to say, is not the end of the story. Last Christmas the letter from Robert was in a different key. The previous year another friend, with a bit more insight and certainly more courage than we had, had finally got fed up and written him a humorous response: a letter full of *congratulations* on his *not* having had a book published, on his *not* having a church packed to the doors every Sunday, on his not being elected to a university professorship... In other words, "Come off it, Robert. Stop looking for ways to make people reject you. Give up the martyr complex, find what you yourself really can be and simply enjoy it. Start living."

Jesus comes to bring us life. Yes, embracing that life may be painful and costly but it's the life, not the pain, which matters. In John's gospel there is the story of Jesus meeting the paralyzed man by the pool of

Bethesda. He has lain there 18 years. Jesus asks him a question which seems so naive, yet it's the most searching question any of us can ever be asked: "Do you *want* to be made well?" The man complains that it's useless – someone else is always into the pool before him when the curative stirring up of the waters occurs and he has no one to help him. No doubt he has recited this lament many times before. He has been programmed into the role of perpetual victim. Perhaps he actually fears being made well again, and entering into life with all its excitements, risks and responsibilities. Jesus' word is stark and plain: "Stand, take your mat, and walk."

It is not only individuals who sometimes want to play the part of victim or martyr. Whole communities can do so as well. Here in Europe, in the ecumenical bodies we have been trying to accompany the churches of Yugoslavia and the Balkans as a whole, caught up in the bitter conflicts of which the recent war in and over Kosovo is but the latest (and we pray the last). We have been seeking to identify and stand with those voices in Serbia, especially in the Serbian Orthodox Church, who have been calling for a new way for their society: a society based on human rights and democracy and acceptance of ethnic and religious diversity, not the way of exclusive ethnic and religious loyalty. Often central to that latter doctrine is the idea of perpetual suffering: "Ever since our glorious defeat in the battle of Kosovo in 1389 we have been the martyred and crucified nation."

No one can deny the real sufferings of a people etched in their history. But to claim the role of eternal victim is tragically unhealthy for a people. It blinds them to the sufferings they in turn inflict upon others, if not actually justifying them. It prevents them from seeing how they can ever be truly responsible for their own destiny within the community of nations. Such a nation, if it is to have any real future, needs the gospel of life to overcome its pathological self-glorification in suffering.

So, some people seem almost to enjoy suffering. Others may not go that far, but tell other people that suffering at the hands of others is just something they should put up with. I am not qualified to speak of what can evidently happen in the dark depths of some human souls who enjoy inflicting suffering on others. But what we should be alert to as Christians is the inbuilt acquiescence in such suffering which some misreadings of the way of the cross have led to. "It's your cross – you just have to bear it" is a word which too often claims justification from today's gospel passage.

The women's desk of the Conference of European Churches has produced a booklet on violence against women in society and churches in Europe today, entitled *It Happens Everywhere – Including Your Community*. It raises uncomfortable issues, it points up harsh facts and above all it tells stories like this one from a woman: "After years of suffering... batterings almost every Friday evening – I used the last drop of my energy and went to my pastor. I felt that I was becoming crazy. Fear and shame had killed my self-esteem. I was breathing, but nothing else was left. The pastor welcomed me, and he gave me this advice: 'Next Friday, think of Jesus who endured so much more anguish for your sake. If you tolerate your earthly burden of suffering, and be sure not to break the marriage vows, you can look forward to joy in heaven.'" To which the only appropriate response is, I believe, "Get behind me, Satan." Jesus does not tell us to meekly accept suffering as an end or virtue in itself. Rather he calls us to embrace the fullness of life which God gives *even if* it means a cross – a very different thing. Embracing the fullness of life includes transforming the violence and the violator through courageous love which is not at all the same as just letting violence have its way. "There are some standing here who will not taste death *before* they see the Son of Man coming in his kingdom."

Let's rejoin Dietrich Bonhoeffer in his prison cell in Berlin. Someone who was certainly bearing the cross, but not making too much of it. Someone who was above all wanting to *live*: rejoicing in God's daily gifts; letters and visits from his fiancée and family; the blackbird singing in a tree outside; the cigar, a present from the theologian Karl Barth; music heard on the radio in the guard-room. Someone who communed with God morning and evening in prayer and meditation on the Bible. Someone who did not dwell on his own discomforts but sought to make life a bit easier for the other prisoners fearing brutality from the guards and death from the allied bombers overhead. Someone who knew that God is always seeking to create the new humanity of love in us, in life, in death, and in life beyond death. Someone who knew that, well before he tasted death with the hangman's rope around his neck, the kingdom of Christ was coming into his life and into his world.

Someone, moreover, who wrote a poem, at new year 1945, by which time he had been transferred to the Gestapo cellars and knew what form his own cross was finally likely to take. He wrote it for those closest to him. It's not a grim acceptance that the cross has to be borne, but an affirmation that God's will for us is life, and wholeness, and joy, and *therefore* the cup of suffering can be drunk too. He wrote it for us as well, and we often sing it in the version which appears in the hymnbook *Thuma Mina*:

> By gracious pow'rs so wonderfully sheltered
> and confidently waiting come what may,
> we know that God is with us night and morning
> And never fails to greet us each new day.

Times and Seasons – and Hope

Acts 1:7: "It is not for you to know times or seasons which the Father has fixed by his own authority."

In the grounds of the Ecumenical Centre, close to the library, there stands a small sundial. On it you will see these words, now somewhat worn by time and weather, inscribed, "To the memory of Joseph H. Oldham 1874-1969 – missionary statesman – foremost pioneer of WCC – friend of Africa." An unobtrusive memorial, going largely unnoticed, it is in fact a very fitting symbol of someone who did so much for the ecumenical movement in the first half of the 20th century, yet who mostly worked behind the scenes, not caring for publicity. The sundial, unlike many clocks, makes no noise. And not only was Joe Oldham quietly spoken. For most of his adult life he had to endure the silent world of his deafness.

The sundial marks the passage of time, each hour of daylight. We who claim to be theologically educated know that the Greek Bible uses two different words for "time". On the one hand, there is *chronos*: sundial time, clock-time, measured in minutes, hours, days, months and years. Today, the *chronos* is 25 May 1998. On the other hand there is the word *kairos*, meaning the time or season for something important to happen. The right time for doing something, which can't be measured by clock-time or the calendar. In England, it is too much of a risk to plant your outdoor tomatoes on 25 May. You have to judge whether summer is really coming and the frosts are over. All of us who have been parents-to-be know that predictions about when the baby is due are never precise. Whatever the doctor has said about the *chronos* of birth, it's when the woman wakes up in the small hours and says, "I think something is happening" that you know the *kairos* of birth has arrived. *Kairos* is the season of crisis and opportunity, when decisive action is called for.

Those of us brought up in Western culture are very much devoted to *chronos*. Just how much, we often discover only when we visit Africa or

---

Sermon preached at Monday morning worship in the Ecumenical Centre, Geneva, 25 May 1998.

Asia. There, it may come as a healthy surprise to us to discover that while the church service or meeting is advertised for 6 o'clock in the evening, it actually starts when the people arrive, whenever that is: and that is the important moment.

It was the theologian Paul Tillich who emphasized the significance of *kairos* as the particular moment in history when we are faced with unprecedented crisis and opportunity. In our lifetime, it was the radical theologians of South Africa who in 1985 spoke so sharply and prophetically of a *kairos* in their country, a country being shaken to the foundations by the conflict between the demand for justice and repression by the state. Since then *kairos* has become almost a theological in-word, and it seems that everywhere from Latin America to Europe, we are called to recognize a *kairos*.

We therefore do well to notice, at the beginning of the Acts of the Apostles, Luke's account of the Ascension. The words of Jesus as he takes leave of his disciples – as it were with one foot still on the earth – include both *chronos* and *kairos*. "It is not for you to know times [*chronous*] or seasons [*kairous*] which the Father has fixed by his own authority." What this tells us, first of all, is that God is concerned with both sorts of time, with clock-time and the season of crisis and opportunity. Both are significant, both are in God's hands, and neither is to be played off against the other. Second, we can measure clock-time, and we might imagine how it will be when a dramatic *kairos* arrives. But we cannot actually know how long the clock-time will last, and when the *kairos* will arrive, above all the final great *kairos* of the *parousia*, the kingdom in all its glorious fullness. The future is God's, and God's alone, to know. Amid endeavours and uncertainties, progress and disappointments, we walk by faith, not by sight. Or, as that troublesome Danish prophet Søren Kierkegaard put it, life can only be understood backwards, but has to be lived forwards.

Which brings me back to Joe Oldham, and his continuing witness to us in the ecumenical movement today. Strains and stresses in the ecumenical movement are nothing new. Indeed, as in mechanics so in ecumenism, perhaps without a certain amount of tension there will be no movement. But more than that, the ecumenical movement almost from its beginning in the 20th century has periodically faced grave threat of rupture. As we are all told, the modern ecumenical movement began with the great world missionary conference at Edinburgh 1910. Joe Oldham was appointed secretary of the continuation committee of Edinburgh. Plans for a more permanent international ecumenical body had not proceeded very far when Europe, and soon much of the rest of the world, was plunged into war in 1914. The churches in the warring nations largely waved their national flags and followed the lines of their respective governments. German and British church leaders accused each other of betraying the Christian cause by their national allegiances. And nowhere was the bitterness deeper than among those who as missionary leaders had been present together in Edinburgh.

The reasons for this bitterness were real. Many of the great German missionary societies had been working in British colonial territories, or in countries soon occupied by the British. There were real dangers that their work, which had such a magnificent record, might be finished for good in an atmosphere where British public opinion, and government policy, now regarded everything German as of the devil. The German missionary leaders protested: where was the voice of British and American Christianity which should be defending Christian missions as lying beyond national interests? They felt betrayed by Oldham, and by John Mott in America. At the time they did not know, could hardly know, that Joe Oldham was quietly working behind the scenes with the British colonial office to ensure that German mission property would not be confiscated and sold off, and that in the long term there would be no restrictions on missionaries of any nationality working in British-ruled territory.

It was a time of deep pain, on both sides. During those dark days of war, Oldham believed more deeply than most that the Christian word must be that of reconciliation, and that reconciliation must come about. But equally, as he tried to tell his German counterparts by letter, that reconciliation would only truly come about when he and they could meet face to face in personal encounter, to forgive and be forgiven. And that moment was not possible yet, while the guns were blazing and the torpedoes were sending lives to the bottom of the sea. It would surely come in God's time. When that time would be could not be predicted, though come it would. Meanwhile there had to be the patient endurance, and the quiet work of laying in place the pieces of the future bridges. The guns did fall silent in November 1918. And before long there were the personal encounters between British, American, French and German Christian and missionary leaders. A new and deeper trust was forged. A *kairos* of new opportunity emerged and was seized with the formation of the International Missionary Council and the other ecumenical bodies. A new ecumenical age dawned, of which we here today are the heirs.

Joe Oldham and others like him are witnesses to faith working in long, drawn-out *chronos* and in discerning the moment of *kairos*: both in waiting and in action; both in patience and in daring venture; both in modest preparation and in seizing the decisive moment of new initiative. In our ecumenical pilgrimage we need both forms of faith, or rather, we should attend to the words of the ascending Jesus, that to both *chronos* and *kairos* are promised the gift of the Spirit. Times and seasons may either surprise or disappoint us: "But you shall receive power when the Holy Spirit has come upon you, and you shall be my witnesses in Jerusalem and Samaria and to the end of the earth." Notice that Jesus is not so much giving us orders here, but rather a promise. He is giving us a gloriously assuring affirmation, that however long and tedious might be the *chronos* we have to work through, or however exciting and demanding the unpredictable *kairos* might be, if we allow the Spirit to work in and through us we shall be witnesses to the coming kingdom. That is the one certainty we have, and need.

Passion and Strategy

Matthew 13:44: "The kingdom of heaven is like treasure hidden in a field, which someone found and hid; then in his joy he goes and sells all that he has and buys that field."

A familiar parable. I think I really began to understand it when I read, not one of the commentaries by any of the great New Testament scholars, not any of your Bultmanns or Jeremias's, but a thriller by that paperback writer of our time Frederick Forsyth: *The Dogs of War*. It is a story about a mineralogist who brings back to London a sample of rock from a mountain somewhere on the coast of west Africa. Laboratory tests show it to consist almost entirely of that rare metal, platinum. At once the story becomes one of intrigue: whoever gets hold of that mountain will make a colossal fortune. It's a billion-dollar mountain. But how to get hold of the mountain? The only way is to get hold of the country in which it is set, for it's obvious that the government of that country, once it finds out what a potential fortune it has, isn't going to let any foreign company or multinational near the place. But how to get hold of the country, which is ruled by a dictator? The only way is to topple him by an armed invasion. So the story escalates from intrigue to gangsterism, arms-running and recruitment of mercenaries and so forth – and all the while keeping the discovery of the billion-dollar mountain of platinum a deadly dark secret.

A most politically incorrect story full of intrigue and thuggery. Yet it's very close to the story Jesus tells. Because once you start to imagine what must have actually happened in the parable, you realize that it is hardly a pious story about a virtuous person. It is a story about passionate joy on the one hand, and intrigue and strategy on the other.

Picture the scene. A peasant farmer is ploughing the field – perhaps not a very attractive field to plough: full of rocks and thorn bushes, and on a slope so that the ox is always veering off to the right and pulling the plough out of line. A most unpromising field which the landowner knows never yields much of a crop but it may as well be tilled every

Sermon preached at the annual assembly of Associations of Lay Academies, Rättvik, Sweden, 4 September 1999.

year. Suddenly the plough judders to a stop as it hits something hard. The ploughman curses, thinking that he's hit yet another rock. He bends down to free the plough and sees that he's hit, not a stone, but a huge earthenware pot. Intrigued, he digs it out – with great difficulty because it's so heavy – breaks open the top, puts his hand in and when he pulls it out cannot believe what he's found: a hoard of golden coins.

His first instinct is to shout at the top of his voice to the men in the next field, "Come and see what I've found!" But he stops himself just in time and begins to think: whoever put this money there years and years ago, it now belongs to the landowner. Perhaps he'd better tell the landowner. But then he thinks again: the landowner is rich enough already. Why should he lay claim to this treasure? The result will only be that he buys up even more land and makes even more poor people destitute. Then he starts to think how great it would be if he owned this field. So he digs an even bigger hole in the ground, hides the pot carefully, and goes on ploughing.

At the end of the day, having untied and fed the ox, he goes and sees the landowner. "Look," he says, rubbing his nose and trying to look diffident, "that field. I know it's not very good land, you've always said it's hardly worth the effort of ploughing... but, well, I've been thinking. I've always fancied a plot of ground of my own. I reckon I could grow something on it. What would your price be?" The landowner is a bit surprised but shrugs his shoulders and says, "OK, if you can raise the money, here's my price."

The man can hardly contain his excitement as he hurries home, but tries to remain calm as he tells his wife he's taking out his small savings, and she's got to sell her one piece of jewellery. Then he goes off to his brothers and brothers-in-law and begs them to lend him however much they have, he will explain it all later. Next day he goes to the landowner, and the field is his. He doesn't do anything about the treasure for a long time, perhaps days, weeks, even a year maybe. He knows where the treasure is, hidden. Then, at the right time, he "finds" it again.

A bit of a cheat, a wily devil, this man whom Jesus holds up to us as an example of how to seek God's kingdom. The kingdom is something to be unbelievably excited about – yet to obtain it means also careful strategy, even cunning. The kingdom is obtained through passionate joy combined with craft. You can't just grab the treasure and run off with it; you have to buy the field in which it lies hidden. Joy and planning. Excitement and patience. Awareness of what is lying there *now,* and *time* to find the right way to having it.

It means a great deal to me to be at the assembly of the Association of Lay Academies in Europe. And I am not speaking first as the general secretary of the Conference of European Churches, though I want to pay tribute to the significance of the Association as a member of CEC. But I speak first as one who owes a great personal debt to the lay academies movement. I can still recall how excited I felt as a theological student over thirty years ago, when I first heard how the institutions in Germany, many of them set up after the second world war, were seeking to bring together Christian faith and the realities of life and responsibility in the secular world, the world in which laypeople were the agents of mission. And a few years later, it was through the laity education movement in Britain that I myself first got involved in theological teaching, when I was asked to develop a programme of laity education in one of our Baptist theological seminaries. That was the generation in Britain inspired by people like Mark Gibbs and Ralph Morton, and it was through the presence at our British meetings of people like Werner Simpfendörfer that I met the full impact of that bold, radical experimentation of faith grappling with secular issues that has been the great contribution of the academies movement to ecumenical life.

The ecumenical movement will always need places which serve the churches and the world, as centres of experimental thought and exploration, related to the churches but with a real degree of independence and freedom to raise the questions which institutions – including ecumenical institutions – often will not or cannot ask: places on the frontier between church and world. And to speak of "frontier" is a cue to mention the other reason why it means much to me to be at Rättvik. "Frontier" was a favourite term of one of the greatest pioneers of the ecumenical movement in the 20th century, J.H. Oldham. Joe Oldham, himself a layperson, was at the centre of nearly all the ecumenical developments of that century, from the Edinburgh world missionary conference of 1910 to the 1937 Oxford Life and Work conference on "Church, Community and State", and the founding of the World Council of Churches, of which he was one of the chief architects. And one of his principal lifelong themes was the need for the laity to be mobilized and empowered for their mission in secular life, and for theological thinking always to be done on that dangerous frontier where the world continually throws up new ethical challenges.

But why Rättvik? Well, it was here that the International Missionary Council (IMC), of which Oldham was chief founder and secretary, met in 1926. It laid plans for the world missionary conference to be held in Jerusalem in 1928. But it was also at that meeting, I believe, that Oldham saw that the IMC, as far as he was concerned, had had its day – in his view, it had become too captive to the conservatism of the Western foreign mission boards. For Oldham the agenda of mission was to be found in the issues of racial justice, in economic order, in the political future of Africa and India, and in the threatening collapse of Western societies themselves. He was looking for another frontier.

Nearly everyone who has ever heard of Oldham knows just one quote from him. In his pioneering book *Christianity and the Race Problem* which appeared in 1924 he declared:

> Christianity is not primarily a philosophy but a crusade. As Christ was sent by the Father, so he sends his disciples to set up in the world the kingdom of God. His coming was a declaration of war – a war to the death against the powers of darkness... Hence when Christians find in the world a state of things that is not in accord with the truth which they have learned from Christ, their concern is not that it should be explained but that it should be ended.

That is *passion* speaking (although if he were alive today we would hope he would use another word than "crusade"), the passion for the kingdom seen as infinitely precious treasure, or the pearl of great price. But Joe Oldham was not only passionate. He was in fact a very quiet person, and moreover afflicted by almost complete deafness for most of his life. He worked carefully, craftily. Some called him "that canny Scot" (most Scots are, of course!); others "a wily prophet". He worked mostly behind the scenes, out of the limelight, in the world of memoranda, small meetings and one-to-one conversations. He worked by getting people together who would not otherwise have met: social scientists, educators, politicians and scientists as well as church leaders and theologians. And he actually made things happen, not least in influencing British policy in Africa in the 1920s and 1930s. He knew that before the treasure of social justice or international peace or better race relations could be achieved, the whole field had to be bought and much hard work and ploughing in the surrounding soil had to be done.

The world of Rättvik today is very different from the world of Rättvik in 1926. But the blend of passion and craft which we see in someone like Oldham, a pioneer in so much of what the academies stand for, is still needed. And it is needed nowhere more urgently than in the search for a Christian contribution to peace-making in Europe today. Kosovo has been humbling for all of us, in the churches and ecumenical bodies no less than in government and NATO and the UN and so on. Some of us have been heavily engaged on behalf of the churches during the crisis, but we cannot pretend to have produced more answers than questions. Maybe we are not even asking the most important questions yet. CEC, with its Roman Catholic partners, remains committed to exploring the idea of a commission on conflict prevention and reconciliation in Europe. But our thinking remains embryonic. We need your help in the academies.

On the one hand, we need the passion, the joyful passion, that there is this great treasure called reconciliation, revealed by the gospel to be embedded in the soil of this world in which Jesus was born and died and was raised to life. The church must proclaim this gospel of peace in the face of resignation and cynicism which accepts as inevitable Europe's propensity to division and conflict. Equally, we need the hard thinking, the craft, the patient strategizing, the selection of priorities and objectives and use of our limited resources if we are to be more than peddlers of unattainable dreams and thereby, in turn, deeper pessimism.

What would I look for the academies to offer here? I can think of several things, and there are probably many more: thinking on specific situations and issues in a more sustained and continuous way than is allowed by the demands of highly publicized short-term programmes which demand quick results; space in which people who would not otherwise meet can encounter each other, especially from situations of actual or potential conflict, without the pressures of playing to the public gallery; discovering hitherto unrecognized resources and possibilities for peace-making in so-called ordinary people; and all linked in a Europe-wide network of sharing insights and information.

I hope and pray that this time together in Rättvik will stimulate you, and in turn all of us in CEC, to open up new possibilities on where our passion and craft might take us. The treasure may be hidden in the field, but our faith tells us that it is real, and the hard and difficult and unpromising field is worth buying with all we have got.

The Living Water:
Uncontrollable Gift of Love

John 4:10: "Jesus answered her, 'If you knew the gift of God, and who it is that is saying to you, "Give me a drink", you would have asked him, and he would have given you living water.'"

4:14: "'... those who drink of the water that I will give them will never be thirsty. The water that I will give will become in them a spring of water gushing up to eternal life.'"

The whole of Europe seems to be on pilgrimage. It's not just that so many have come to Nidaros in these days for the St Olav festival, but that so many other events have been taking place where people are revisiting the saints and holy places, especially here in the Nordic region. Last month Sweden was also celebrating King Olav's baptism at the well of Husaby, Finland was celebrating the 700th anniversary of Turku cathedral, and some of us were present in Iceland for the 1000th anniversary of Christianity in that westernmost country of Europe.

Such anniversaries, and the start of a new millennium, have been prompting us to revisit those places and people of the past. And it is interesting how often such people and places, one way or another, are associated with water. One of the great saints of Britain, St David the patron saint of Wales, was known as David the lover of water, because he stressed simplicity of life and the importance of "little things", of which water is the greatest example. Water has a profound meaning for nearly all of us as Christians because it is in water that we are baptized into the new life in Christ: whether with a lot of water, as in my own Baptist tradition, or with a more inhibited use of it, as in most other churches. It thus represents also our fundamental unity in Christ: water from different wells and reservoirs may taste slightly differently because of a variety of salts and minerals in it, but fundamentally it is still the same water that we all need. So there was rich meaning in that simple ceremony early on in our worship service, when water from many parts of Europe was poured together into one vessel.

Sermon preached at an outdoor ecumenical service on St Olav's Day, 29 July 2000, Trondheim, Norway.

At the heart of the beautiful story in St John's gospel, of Jesus and the woman of Samaria at the well of Jacob, is "living water". In the East, certainly in the time of Jesus, people would speak of well-water as "living water" because it seeped into the well of its own accord, unlike the water in a tank or cistern which has to be put there by human effort. I was once travelling across the desert in the land of Jordan, and we came to a small settlement of ancient buildings dating right back to Roman times, if not earlier. In the centre of the settlement was a well. It was a kind of miracle, that in the midst of this dry, barren wilderness, seemingly totally waterless, you could look down this shaft in the ground and there, gleaming as it reflected the sky, was water. It somehow came there out of the surrounding rock and sand, of its own accord, as though it was alive. So Jesus is in a way playing on words when he says to the Samaritan woman, "If you knew the gift of God, and who I am, I could give you living water, even though I haven't a bucket and the well is deep." It's life which comes as a gift from God, what we call *grace*: the gift which comes unexpectedly and without our deserving it or ever being good enough to merit it. That is the heart of the gospel.

One of the important recent ecumenical advances has been the agreement, signed in Augsburg on Reformation Day in October 1999, between the Lutheran World Federation and the Roman Catholic Church, on the issue of "justification". It was conflict over this doctrine which ruptured Western Christianity in the 16th century and has been a source of dispute ever since. Now, both world communions are saying: for our salvation we look entirely to the grace of God which we receive in faith and not to any merit in ourselves.

That is basic to the Christian message. It must always be a note for people to hear from the church. It is a message which delivers us from despair: there is always the offer of life for us, however wretched we may feel, however low we may think we have sunk. Equally, it's a message which counters our pride and arrogance when we think we ourselves, or our church or our nation are good enough, clever enough, or know enough or are religious enough, to save ourselves and tell others how to behave.

In this respect, water has acquired some tragic associations in Christian history. Had I the chance, I would have liked to bring some water for the opening ceremony, as reminders that our use of water has not always pointed to the grace and love of God but to human self-righteousness and intolerance and injustice. I would like, for example, to have brought some water from the river Limmat at Zurich, where in the 16th century the first leaders of the Anabaptist movement were condemned and drowned, on the orders of the "official" reformer Zwingli.

Or to have brought from Thingvellir in Iceland some of that water from the pool beneath the icy waterfall, where in the 17th century women found guilty of immoral conduct were drowned – but not the men. We bring water of repentance for cleansing and renewal.

We all live by *grace*. None of us can live long without needing to drink the water which comes to us from outside ourselves, like water into the well. That keeps us both hopeful and humble.

But there's another way in which water can be "living water". Even more vibrantly alive than water seeping into a well is the water which spurts up from a spring, like St Olav's spring just down the hill from here, or which sparkles into the air as a fountain. In Geneva where I live we have a splendid fountain, the *Jet d'eau*, set in the lake by the water-front. It soars like a huge white feather many metres high into the air. But it sometimes causes problems. On days when the wind is blowing strong from the north-east it has to be shut down, otherwise much of the city will be given a cold shower. That's the problem with really living water – especially when the wind blows: it can't be controlled. You don't know where it might end up. Jesus tells the woman that the water he gives will gush up like a spring to eternal life: that is life which is endless because it knows no boundaries. It is God's own life in us, and therefore eternal as God is eternal. It is love, as God is love, love without limits, love without end; love welling up into our world and blown by the Spirit wherever it wills. God gives us new life as a gift, but it is an uncontrollable gift once we allow it to flow through us.

The ecumenical movement is not so much about reorganizing the churches as disorganizing them, about breaking down the walls between us so that the living water of love created by the Holy Spirit can flow among us, and out through us to a thirsty world. The living water is a current of reconciliation, and one sign of its flowing is whenever hardened attitudes and assumptions are questioned and challenged. Right at the beginning of our gospel story we see how Jesus himself lives in a way which totally disregards the social barriers and prejudices of the time. He asks the Samaritan woman for a drink, and she is taken aback by this: "How is it that you, a Jew, ask a drink of me, a Samaritan woman?"

At that time, the Samaritans and the Jews despised each other. As so often where communities are at enmity with each other, there was a long story behind it. Seven centuries earlier, the northen half of Israel was swallowed up by the all-conquering Assyrian empire. Many of the people were deported, and replaced by foreign settlers who brought their own religions with them. So in the course of time the people of Samaria were looked down upon by the Jews of Jerusalem who thought them racially and religiously corrupt, not real Israelites at all. They tried to have as little to do with each other as possible, and for Jews to sit at the same table as Samaritans or use the same cups and dishes would be unthinkable. It would make them "unclean". As for Samaritan *women*, some of the comments from Jewish religious teachers of the time are virtually unprintable. Well might the Samaritan woman be surprised, then, when this Jewish man asks for a drink from her bottle.

Notice, Jesus doesn't preach a sermon about inter-racial or interfaith harmony. He simply lives in a way which ignores the customs and conventions and enmity, as a stream in full flood overflows its banks. He behaves towards the Samaritan woman as he might towards his own sister. He is simply a thirsty human being, and she another human being who can give him a drink. But he is a thirsty human being who is God's eternal Word made flesh, God made as human as we are and so here for everyone. When the water of life is here, true human unity is restored, because all need it, and it is offered to everyone. There will be another time when Jesus says, "Please give me a drink." He will not be sitting by a well, but hanging on a cross, at the point where he gives himself: love giving all, for all that is. It is from his wounds that there flows the living water, for everybody without distinction: Jew and Samaritan, male and female, Greeks and barbarians, white and black, Norwegian and Sami, citizens at home and asylum-seekers from far away, religious and unreligious people, saints and sinners.

One of the great Orthodox saints and theologians of the middle ages, Symeon the "New Theologian", reflecting on the wonder of the incarnation, the self-giving and self-humbling of the Son of God become human and dying on a cross, speaks of "a God without pride". A God without pride: one who is not afraid to admit being thirsty and to ask a drink from anyone without questions about religion or race or social status or gender or ritual cleanness. I wonder what would happen if each of us here was to take some further step, however small, of living this way, a way consistent with being refreshed by the living water of God's love? You never know what might happen, eventually, for "truth and reconciliation".

Some sixty or so years ago, a young black boy growing up in a South African township was learning that, as far as the rulers of his country were concerned, he and all other black children were second- or third-class citizens, looked down upon or ignored by white people generally, and there seemed little hope for any real justice or change in attitude. But one or two things kept hope alive in him that things might be different. One very simple thing was the way in which the white Anglican priest serving that poor neighbourhood would always raise his hat when greeting his mother, an almost unheard of thing for a white man to do when meeting a black woman, like a Jewish man asking a drink of a Samaritan woman. But it always happened: "Good morning, Mrs Tutu"; and young Desmond was always impressed.

Jesus brings us the living water of God's love: a gift, an uncontrollable gift when we let it flow to us and through us. Here on St Olav's day we praise God for Olav and for all the men and women who have let themselves in turn become wells and fountains of God's grace in our world. May we be refreshed by their example, and by our own experience of the living water. May we be strengthened as we return to the wells from which they drank, and as we continue on our pilgrimage to find the new ones still waiting to be discovered along our way. Thanks be to God.

Tradition? Watch Out for Saints!

Ephesians 2:14: "For he is our peace... and has broken down the dividing wall, that is, the hostility between us."

As we walked in procession through the streets of Trondheim at the start of the St Olav festival, with flags flying and bands playing, I found myself thinking, "What a good thing it is to feel you have a tradition; and how lucky the people of Trondheim are to have the great story of St Olav at the centre of their tradition." A sense of tradition can give us strength and purpose, as a community, a church, a nation.

Not everyone will agree with this. Some will argue that a sense of tradition keeps us locked in the past, whereas it is here and now we have to live, today's challenges we have to face instead of fighting again the battles of long ago, whether Stikelstadt where Olav died in 1030, or wherever. That is important to remember, too.

So people can get very passionate about tradition, either defending it or attacking it. But sometimes, whether we are for it or against it, what we imagine to be "traditional" turns out to be rather different from how things actually were in the past. The school which our two sons attended is the cathedral school in the city of Bristol in the west of England. It is a very old school, and being attached to the cathedral some of its buildings date right back to the middle ages. A few years ago, the school authorities decided to embark on a programme of extending and modernizing some of the premises. When they submitted their plans to the city council planning authority, for purposes of fire precautions they were required to add an extra door, which would have to be put in one of the ancient walls. When local conservationists heard about this they were up in arms: that wall, they argued, had stood like that for the best part of a thousand years. To place a modern fire-escape door in it would be sacrilege.

The debate went on, the needs of modern fire-safety versus the wish to preserve the historic past, and higher government authority finally had

Sermon preached at the Bakke (Lutheran) church, Trondheim, Norway, on the occasion of the St Olav festival, 29 July 2001.

to decide. It decided, finally, in favour of the fire-door. So the workmen eventually got to work on the medieval wall. They had not got very far in chiselling away the outer layer of rubble and plaster when they discovered a large hole. It turned out to be a door-shaped hole. In fact, it *was* a door, a medieval door, right at that spot where the new door was meant to be. Traditionalists and modernizers had been arguing passionately about a door, when all along, covered up by later rubble, there was a door there all the time. Underneath our assumptions and prejudices the real past can have surprises in store for us.

Traditions can themselves be walls which divide and separate people off from each other. Because they can be a source of gratitude and pride, they can also easily become reasons for people to feel superior to others, generating prejudice, bigotry and even violence. Recently I was in Belfast in Northern Ireland, at the start of what they call the "marching season" there. People from the "nationalist" and "loyalist" communities were again busy throwing bricks and petrol bombs at each other and the police. The peace process seems as fragile as ever. What is sad, of course, is that on both sides so many people who appeal to their "tradition", whether Catholic or Protestant, have little idea of what those traditions actually mean. So often they are a concoction of half-truths and myths.

This is where the "saints" can be especially important to us. Many of the saints venerated in Europe today are associated with particular holy places, like St Olav here in Trondheim. Or St Thomas à Becket in Canterbury, or St Francis at Assisi, or St Theresa at Avila. Saints and martyrs are nearly always linked with special places. But the interesting thing is that they nearly always have a wider appeal than those particular places. Their attraction is not limited to their home town, or home country, or their own church. And while they may have resided mainly in one or a few places, while their shrine may be preserved and cherished in one place, the great saints do not just belong to their own country or church. They are not owned by, they are not the private property of, their native country or church. Saintliness, true holiness, makes an appeal which crosses all national, racial and confessional boundaries.

Today, as we rediscover the value of pilgrimage to places associated with saintly women and men, so we rediscover the fact that in the centuries before Europe divided itself up into separate and rigidly defined nation-states, the great pilgrim-centres of Europe drew people from far and wide, from all nationalities and languages, from Santiago de Compostela in the south to Nidaros here in the north. The saints and their shrines were not national properties, but were cherished in common by all the Christian peoples of Europe. Sainthood was not a wall separating people off from each other, a wall to be preserved intact at all costs, but a doorway through which all people could pass into fuller experience of life with God.

Saints are those who point us to Christ, *the* holy one of God. If we are to talk about "tradition" as Christians, there is only one tradition that at the end of the day really matters: the tradition about Jesus himself. There is only one traditional custom that is to be preserved at all costs, the one that we are about to observe as we come to the Lord's table, and hear again the apostle Paul's words handing on to us in turn the command to break bread and drink from the cup, in memory of our Lord's death, in recognition of his risen presence, and in hope of his coming glory. He is our peace – he has broken down the dividing wall between us. In him we rediscover the door so often covered up by our man-made traditions of custom and prejudice. For the apostle Paul the wonderful truth of the gospel was that the dividing wall between the Jewish and gentile worlds of his time had been breached by Christ, for both had been brought near to God in a new way through the death of Jesus on the cross. Whether we are Jew or gentile, whether Norwegian or German, whether white or black, in the light of the cross we know ourselves all to be sinners, all to be loved by God, all to be offered God's forgiveness, all invited to become members of his one new family in the beloved Son, all to be part of the one new humanity in place of the old divisions and hostilities.

"Jesus Christ Heals and Reconciles – Our Witness in Europe": in June 2003, you will see those words all over Trondheim. They are the theme of the next assembly of the Conference of European Churches, which will be meeting here. We are hoping for up to 700 participants from all the churches of Europe, east and west, north and south, Protestant and Orthodox and Anglican, with Roman Catholic observers as well. "Jesus Christ Heals and Reconciles – Our Witness in Europe" – it is a very bold theme. But we hope that coming to Trondheim will in itself inspire us to take these words seriously, as in the city of St Olav, one of the great pan-European Christian figures of the past, we rediscover more of our common European Christian heritage. As we well know, the old wall of division in Europe symbolized by the Berlin wall has gone, but new divisions seem constantly threatening to reappear, from Northern Ireland to the Balkans, and not just between peoples but increasingly within our societies as well. At Trondheim in 2003, we want to be inspired both to receive and to give the new hope for Europe given by the gospel.

Saints are those who by their example hold open for us doors of healing and reconciliation. They are living signs that the grace of Jesus

Christ, himself the great opening through walls of estrangement and hostility, can and does work in our lives and in our world. For a picture of this I look to the great rose window in Nidaros cathedral in Trondheim. Its centre is blood-red. Radiating out from it like spokes of a wheel are arms of tracery which at their ends each enclose glass of different colours and symbols. I think of these as the saints produced by Christ who is the centre, who is our peace. They come from him, they radiate out from him, but also point back towards him, the blood-red centre of incarnate love. They are those whom Christ calls to share his work of opening up doorways, of breaking down barriers. That means you and me as well, for we are all, in our own way, "called to be saints", and the ongoing task of healing, peace-making and reconciliation is the most worthwhile tradition of all.

The Love That Makes
All Things New

Revelation 21:3: "And I heard a loud voice from the throne saying, 'Behold, the home of God is among mortals. He will dwell with them as their God; they will be his peoples, and God himself will be with them.' And he who sat on the throne said, 'See, I am making all things new.'"

I am not one of those who expect the world to end when the clock strikes twelve next new year's eve, even if the computers have problems. But I do feel a twinge of excitement at the thought of the first time I shall write a letter and put the date at the top with "2000".

People in the ancient world used to reckon years and days by whoever was ruler at the time, emperors and local governors. For the first generations of Christians that presented an interesting question: Who is the real ruler of this world? In the early years of the 2nd century (as we now call it) the Christian church at Smyrna in Asia Minor (today's Turkey) suffered a tragic loss. It was a time of persecution, when the Roman emperor suddenly decreed that everywhere in the empire important people should prove their loyalty to him, by offering incense to him as to a god. At Smyrna the old and revered leader of the church, Polycarp by name, was singled out by the Roman governor to pass this test. Polycarp refused, saying that for nigh on 80 years he had followed Jesus as Lord and did not see any reason to deny him now. So Polycarp was put to death. The Christians at Smyrna wrote to their neighbouring churches about this event, and this is how they dated it: "The martyrdom of Polycarp took place during the Proconsulship of Statius the 4th, *but in the everlasting reign of Jesus Christ.*"

The everlasting reign of Jesus Christ. For Christians, that is the only date that really matters. Emperors and governors may come and go, and do their worst (or their best for that matter), but Jesus Christ is Lord. History will in the end prove to be *his story*, and his victory. That is a breathtaking claim to make, with your backs to the wall and your faces to the sword.

Sermon preached at an ecumenical service in Clare, Suffolk, England, during the Week of Prayer for Christian Unity, 24 January 1999.

I am fairly sure that one thing that would have helped the Christians of Smyrna was that about a generation earlier, they themselves had received a letter. It came to them, and to six other churches in their part of the world. It too had been written in a time of great persecution, when the then emperor had been wanting to stamp his supreme authority on everyone and everything. Christians were dying by the score, or being tortured or being forced into labour under barbarous conditions in the salt-mines. It seemed as though all was up with the Christian movement, and the future lay only with the march of the legions and the worship of power. It was a long letter, with a lot of strange language about stars falling from heaven, and beasts rising from the abyss and being thrown down again. All this was a coded message, such as resistance movements often use. Its basic message was clear: despite all that is happening, behind all that is happening, our God reigns. And the end is his victory.

That letter is what we now call the Book of Revelation, written by a man called John, punished for his faith by lonely exile on the little island of Patmos. He had had a strange and wonderful vision, which he believed came straight from the risen Lord Jesus himself. Instead of keeping it for himself he wanted to share it with his fellow Christians, to bring them encouragement, so that they would stand firm in the faith that, come what may, God reigns and God's final purpose will triumph. And towards the end of his letter, he spells it out with the words from our text and others like them. A new heaven and a new earth, a new holy city radiant with light and beauty. The good news that God will dwell with humans and they with him forever, of death and crying and pain being no more, "for the former things have passed away".

I am glad that the Christians of Malaysia, who have prepared the material for this year's Week of Prayer for Unity, have chosen this passage for the main theme as we approach the new millennium. It is good because when the word "new" is on everyone's lips as it is just now, it is important to ask, "Just what makes anything really new?" What is true newness? We will soon get used to writing 2000 instead of 1999. And so we seriously expect real change in our world just because the dates have changed? And it is a question addressed to our faith as well. Do we really believe the former things will have passed away: death and mourning and crying and pain?

Just last week, I was in southern Italy visiting churches there who are trying to witness to the gospel in the midst of some of the worst poverty in Europe. My hosts took me to a district of Naples called Ponticelli, not far from the foot of Mt Vesuvius. Where the unemployment rate is something like 40 percent. Where probably the majority of young people are on drugs. Where girls lured from Africa or Eastern Europe by promises of jobs in smart restaurants are made to work as prostitutes. Where, so the head of the local hospital told me, the two most common reasons for people coming into the hospital are liver diseases caused by living in such polluted and unhygienic surroundings, and gunshot wounds thanks to the local mafia. Standing there, amid these bleak high-rise blocks littered with rubbish in between, you feel like saying: "Damn the London Millennium Dome and all that trivial claptrap! What will end the death and the crying and pain that desecrate human life here?"

Some people will say, "Ah, but what really is making our world new is the new technology, especially the technology of communication which is really making our world one world in an unprecedented way." Yes, it is great to have e-mail and be on the internet and converse with friends and colleagues – and even people you don't know – all over the world in an instant. The internet *is* great – *if* you're on it. But most people are not, and never will be. By themselves, our wonderful new ways of communicating will not end the old order, because one main feature of the old order is perpetuated: the exclusion of so many people. Globalization, that umbrella word that covers everything from electronic communication to the worldwide market economy to MacDonalds restaurants, gives the impression of uniting the world in a new way – but it is an illusion, because it works only by excluding vast numbers of people who are downtrodden, exploited or simply ignored. Ponticelli is just one example of the excluded. We can find others in Africa, or Latin America – or in Britain.

How different is the vision we are given by John of the Revelation! God wills to dwell with all people, to be their God and for them to be his people. He wills to pour forth his abundant grace like life-giving waters, flowing lavishly without end and without limit. In this new holy city, all are included who long for life. If we read on to later passages, it is a city where the gates never shut, where all who wish to participate in its goodness are welcome. It is a vision of inclusion. Walls and barriers are a thing of the past. How can we talk about separation and exclusion any more, when the almighty and holy one simply wants to live with the mortals – that is, the likes of you and me and everyone else – and for them to live with God?

To underline the point, John uses a specially interesting Greek word in saying that "the dwelling" or "the home" of God is with humans or mortals. Literally, the word means "God has pitched his tent" among mortals. It recalls the story of the people of Israel in their desert wanderings, when the glory of God resided in the tabernacle, the tent of God's presence in the midst of the people. What a strange and wonderful picture it is, then, of this new Jerusalem: a city beautiful beyond compare, where God's own self lives not in a palace, still less a battle-mented castle, or behind bullet-proof glass, and not even in a church, but in a frail tent. So close, so accessible to all.

But that should not really surprise if we recall the gospel story. For it is the same word that we were hearing just a month ago as we heard the Christmas readings, and listened to the first chapter of St John's gospel where there is unfolded to us the wonder of the incarnation: "And the word became flesh and *pitched his tent* among us." He pitched his skin-thin tent consisting of a frail human being among other human beings: He was accessible, not just to the religious people who thought they could be proud of their nearness to God, but to all without exclusion, and especially to those who thought they might be excluded: the tax-collec-tors and sinners, the women considered to be unclean, the little children, the people with nasty skin diseases, the people broken and troubled, the poor, the foreigners. He died outside the city wall so that in love he might embrace the city in its entirety. And now he comes right back into the new city to pour forth that life in a never ending, limitless stream.

The vision given to us by John of the Revelation is a vision of this same incarnate love triumphing at the end, with all people and for all people: universal light and ever-flowing water of life, swallowing up death and pain and grief for ever. That is our great hope, affirmed every time we say the creed: We believe in the resurrection of the body and the life everlasting. We cannot fully conceive what it will be like. Still less can we ourselves bring it about. What we are called to, however, is to live in a way which even here and now is consistent with this great faith and hope. A cup of water – note how Jesus speaks of giving just cups of water – is as much water as are the Victoria Falls.

That means, in what ways can we here and now be signs of this great purpose of God for our world, the love that really makes things new? I go back to Ponticelli in Naples. To those small churches which run a hos-pital, which offer care for young people and mothers and unemployed people without distinction. No, they can't change that desperate situation overnight. But they do offer a sign of that love which accepts people, which does not exclude for any reason. They bring an element of what is really new: the love that takes the place of others. That is real newness.

The Week of Prayer for Christian Unity is a great occurrence every year. The movement for Christian unity is a great movement of our time. If I didn't think so, I would not be in my present job. In many ways it does signify a new development. There are those among us who will recall that not so many years ago it would have been thought impossible that Anglicans, Baptists, Roman Catholics and United Reformed people would be worshipping together as we are doing. But if the movement for Christian unity is to be a sign of *God's* newness in our world, we cannot be satisfied with it only as a means of bringing churches closer together.

One of the "old things" in our world is tribalism: the belief that safety and value and meaning are found only in your particular group, which is to be set over against all other groups and the world at large. There is the tribalism of the tribe itself in places like Africa; there is the tribalism of the nation; of the class, of the race or ethnic group. There is also the tribe of the religion or of the church; and all too often in our time religion has been co-opted into one form or other of tribalism. We have seen it in Rwanda and Burundi; in Europe we have seen it in the former Yugoslavia. And Christian unity betrays the gospel if all that results is a kind of ecumenical tribalism over against the world: a way of saying, "We Christians must club together in face of this wicked modern world." If we are inspired by the Revelation vision, the vision of Jesus triumphant who died and lives for all, we shall want to be together for a greater reason than that. Archbishop William Temple once said that the church is the one club that exists for the sake of those who do not belong to it. We shall want to be together for the sake of the world, for the sake of people who not only do not belong to our particular church but do not belong to any church at all. But they belong to God's world, the human world from which God wants to wipe all tears, to take away death and crying and pain.

The word "ecumenical" is itself worth looking at again. It comes from a word in the Greek-speaking world in which Christianity grew up. The word is *oikoumene*. It meant "the whole inhabited earth": the world wherever people are living. So when the early Christians had an "ecumenical" meeting it was a meeting or a council when leaders came from the whole *oikoumene*, which meant for them more or less the whole Roman empire, from draughty Hadrian's wall to the burning sands of North Africa. So, being ecumenical means not just coming together as Anglicans and Baptists and Catholics and so on, but coming together for the sake of the whole inhabited world of which we are part, for the sake of the gospel, the good news which is for this world in its death and crying and pain.

John of Patmos was not the first, nor the last, person to suffer for his testimony to Jesus, and who in suffering was brought to a greater vision. I'm often inspired by that great servant of God in the 20th century, who also spent years in lonely exile in prison for his testimony to Jesus: Pastor Martin Niemöller of Germany in the 1930s was the leading preacher against the attempts to make the church an arm of the Nazi state. As a result he spent nearly eight years in concentration camps. To people all over the world he became a great symbol of Christian resistance to tyranny, and afterwards a great ecumenical leader in the World Council of Churches. At the assembly of the World Council of Churches in Harare in 1998, as we celebrated the 50th anniversary of the WCC, he was among those heroes and heroines of the faith whom we remembered in gratitude to God. But Niemöller once said something about why he was imprisoned which is always deeply challenging and haunting, and a warning against Christian tribalism. He said: "First they [the Nazis] came for the communists, and I was not a communist, so I did not speak out. Then they came for the trades unionists, and I was not a trades unionist, so I did not speak out. Then they came for the Jews, and I was not a Jew, so I did not speak out. Finally they came for me, and there was no one left to speak for me."

"Churches Together" has become a favourite way of calling ecumenical activity in the past few years, in Britain at least. It is good. "Churches Together in Clare". But how about "Churches together FOR Clare" – Churches Together *for* England, *for* Britain and Ireland, *for* the whole world? Churches Together for the sake of whoever is caught up in death and crying and pain? In southern Italy, it is not easy to be ecumenical: the Protestant churches are such a small minority in a largely Catholic environment. Suspicions and resentments are harboured on both sides. But they are also keeping the Week of Prayer for Unity as we are doing. And what really brings them together is not closeness for its own sake, but for the sake of the crying and pain in places like Ponticelli: for example, when Protestants and Catholics join together in a campaign to try to encourage people to resist intimidation by the mafia. It is when the churches together see the needs around them as more important than themselves that a unity comes about which does bring something new, the love which crosses boundaries and barriers for the sake of others.

I find the most astonishing thing about John of the Revelation's vision is that just at the moment when he himself might have been expected to have turned in on himself in self-concern and self-pity, the living Lord Jesus opened his eyes to see the transformation of all things, a whole new heaven and earth. Sometimes I am asked what is my vision for the churches of Europe. I would say: "A Christianity without fear. Churches lifted up beyond fears for themselves and their own prestige and survival, by the perfect love which casts out fear. Churches which witness to real newness by the new kind of love seen in Jesus, the love which reaches out and pitches its tent with others, takes the place of others, bears others' burdens and *speaks for others* in their crying and pain, regardless of who they are."

Real newness will come not just with a new millennium, but with the love of Jesus which takes the place of others and wants to include all others. Friends, we are here together because we believe in the end when, beyond all millennia, God will dwell with us all and we with God, and death and crying and pain will be no more. Let us, in our coming together, seek by God's grace for ways of here and now being signs that that will be the end; ways, however humble and simple but real, of showing the love that lives with others and leaves no one out.

Unity: Hope for the Coming Glory

John 2:9b-10: "... the steward called the bridegroom and said to him, 'Everyone serves the good wine first, and then the inferior wine after the guests have become drunk. But you have kept the good wine until now.'"

This great cathedral has many stories to tell. Here is just one of them. It happened getting on for fifty years ago. A small boy living in Darlington, not far from here, was brought by his mother to spend a day of the Easter holidays here in Durham. From the bus station they made straight for the cathedral. At school he had been told all about St Cuthbert and the Venerable Bede, and was ready to be impressed, and after gazing respectfully at the sanctuary knocker they came inside. But nothing of what he had learnt in history lessons quite prepared him for what he felt as he first stood among these columns and arches. At that tender age he would have found it hard to put his feelings into words. But he would probably have said something like: "It's huge, almost frightening, but at the same time somehow friendly." And although he sensed that here was a place breathing of the dim and distant past, he would also have said something like: "This is a place where something strange might also be *about* to happen."

Well, that small boy has always been grateful for that early experience, and today he would like to say thank you to the dean and the cathedral community for the invitation to be here on behalf of the Conference of European Churches, and on this Sunday in the Week of Prayer for Christian Unity to share in the ministry of the word.

"This is a place where something strange might also be about to happen": the child's sensibility is often the most spiritually instructive, certainly if we take seriously what Jesus said about children. It is not a sense which the churches of Europe, by and large, seem to convey today. To the majority of Europeans at the start of the third Christian millennium the churches are just museums of the past: beautiful maybe, fascinating maybe, reassuring maybe as landmarks of cultural tradition

Sermon preached in Durham Cathedral, England, 23 January 2000, during the Week of Prayer for Christian Unity.

– but not places where something strange, new and wonderful is to be expected.

Yet we have been living through times when new and strange things can happen, even in churches, even in Europe. Thirteen years ago, in 1987, I visited Moscow for the first time. It was winter, and moreover the cold war was not yet over even though we were learning those Russian words "glasnost" and "perestroika". I was shown round the churches and palaces of the Kremlin. Going into the cathedral of the Annunciation was a deeply moving experience: silent, empty, for decades not a place of worship but just a museum of Orthodox art. All around, and above, the figures and icons of saints and angels seemed to be keeping watch, waiting, waiting... for what? Two years ago this month I was in Moscow again, and on Sunday morning in that very same church which was now thronged with people as Patriarch Alexei celebrated the liturgy, and the air was filled with the glorious harmonies of Orthodox chants and clouds of incense. The saints and angels had not watched and waited in vain, and you felt that they too were now singing.

Strange and wonderful new things can happen, not always when we want: sometimes later, sometimes sooner, than we expect or wish. To be prepared for surprises is faith, the hope-filled faith which should inspire our prayers and work for Christian unity. It is a faith and a hope which has to do continual battle with our persistent human inclination to measure everything by what has been or what we imagine has been in the past. Europe today, for all the brave talk about the new millennium, is gripped by a widespread nostalgia. Perhaps that is not surprising, at a time marked by rapid changes, tensions and even conflicts. When the ground trembles beneath us, we want stability, order, certainty such as we imagined always held sway in former times. Someone visiting Hungary a year or two ago told me how an old man had been complaining about all the changes and confusions of the present and said that he much preferred the old order. "You mean you want the communists back?" asked my friend. "I'm not talking about the communists," said the man, "I mean the Hapsburgs" – last heard of in 1918.

That is an attitude not unknown in the churches themselves, and even, I have to admit, in ecumenical bodies these days. A year or two ago, staff at the World Council of Churches in Geneva were invited to take part in a survey of what it was like to work there, the good things and the not-so-good things. One question was, "What would you say is our greatest asset?" One person, with tongue in cheek, answered, "Our glorious past." A bit cynical perhaps, but registering the sense that in the ecumenical movement, at least as represented in Geneva, the best has already been. Everyone talks about the great leading figures of former days: the Visser 't Hoofts, the George Bells, the Suzanne de Diétrichs. People talk with pride not about what they are doing now, but what was done in the great days of the founding assemblies, the earth-shaking developments like the Programme to Combat Racism which was so important for change in Southern Africa, or the times when the Orthodox churches were eager to join the World Council, not like now when some of them are debating whether to stay in. What is there really still to look forward to?

At the wedding feast in Cana of Galilee, the steward who reports on the extraordinarily good quality of the wine now being served expresses the usual order of things: "Everyone serves the good vintage first, and then the cheap stuff from the local off-licence once everyone is over the safe limit for donkey-driving back home. But you have kept the good wine until now." John the Evangelist tells us many things, at many levels rich in imagery, in this story. One thing he is *not* saying is that Jesus is to be seen as a wonder-working magician. Mere wonder-workers do not really change anything; they simply supply sensational happenings at which people goggle for a while and then move on, looking for even more sensational displays. By contrast, Jesus has come to reveal to us who God really is, and what we can become with God.

To get the point of the story, and of all the signs which Jesus performs in John's gospel, we have to remember what John tells us in his first chapter, the passage we heard a few weeks ago at Christmas, about the Word becoming human flesh and dwelling among us so that we behold his glory, glory of the Father's only Son, full of grace and truth: the grace of God's free and boundless love for us; the truth that he really does bring us to communion with himself, sharing his own eternal life as his children, setting us free to reflect his own freely loving nature in our own lives, lives now and eternally. Prayer for Christian unity is prayer for this to happen without limits in the church and in the world.

This grace and truth, the glory of God come among us, comes as surprise, unexpected and undeserved, strange and new, confounding our expectations. Or rather, confounding our lack of expectations. We think we have had the good wine already, until we have tasted *this* surpassing vintage. We think we know what life is all about and what the world is like; we think, maybe, we even know what religion is, until we have drunk of this grace and truth. That is why John includes what would otherwise seem to be purely incidental detail about the six stone water jars for the Jewish rites of purification, which Jesus commands to be filled to the brim with water. The revered ceremonial rites of the traditional religion cannot themselves bring grace and truth, are not in themselves the glory of God. They too need to be taken and transformed by the miracle of divine grace, and included in today's collect when we ask God to "transform the poverty of our nature by the riches of your grace".

Christians should therefore beware of using this aspect of the story as a way of belittling the faith of Judaism. We should rather ask ourselves how much of our patterns of Christianity have themselves become as uninspiring as empty stone jars, the churches as monuments to the past. We and our churches are in continual need of transforming and renewing grace. The searching and praying for the unity of Christians and churches means searching and praying for their renewing and transformation, continually asking "come, Holy Spirit" so that they might experience and become signs of the new creation. It is said of the great saint of 14th-century Russia, Sergius of Radonezh, who founded a community in the wildest part of the forest: "St Sergius built the Church of the Holy Trinity as a mirror for his community, that through gazing at the divine unity they might overcome the hateful divisions of this world."

It means being ready to learn and experience new things – often, from one another. Every step forward along the pilgrimage of unity has involved Christians of different confessions being prepared to be surprised and enriched and humbled by each other, and to receive grace and truth through one another. During Pastor Martin Niemöller's imprisonment the Nazi authorities one day had the idea of making Protestants and Catholic clergy share the same cells. They would surely debate and disagree and accuse each other of being heretics and so their morale would be broken. So Niemöller was put with two Catholic priests. Far from having their morale broken, the three seemed in even better spirits after some weeks. All that had happened was that the Catholics had learnt a lot more about the Bible from Niemöller, and Niemöller had learnt a lot more about how to pray from the Catholic breviary.

Praying for unity means never being wholly satisfied with what we have drunk already, it means expecting the best wine which is still to come. It was therefore a great moment in Rome this past week when, at the Church of St Paul's without the Walls, Pope John Paul II celebrated the millennial jubilee by the opening of the "holy door". The archbishop of Canterbury was with him, and so were many other leading church representatives from Europe and other parts of the world. Pope John Paul made an impassioned plea for further unity, of which this gathering was a sign of hope. There were also notable absences, especially from the Protestant world. There was mingled joy, and hope, and pain. We are not yet at the final great wedding banquet of the Lamb with his bride, the completed and perfected community of God's people which this morning's reading from the book of Revelation portrays. But the best vintage which will be served at that great feast is already being offered us in a preliminary wine tasting.

We are already getting a taste of that best wine whenever, and wherever, and however, we are allowing the grace and truth of God's love in Christ to transform us and bring even a new glimmer of God's glory into our world. Talking with colleagues in Geneva who had been at the holy door ceremony in Rome, I am assured it was a brilliant and moving occasion. I would in many ways have liked to have been there. But I have known other ecumenical events in Italy which were no less revealing of the glory of God, even though they did not take place in a great church with splendid liturgy, as I found just a year ago when was visiting the south of Italy, the urban sprawl of Naples and its desperately poor suburbs under Mt Vesuvius, stricken with unemployment, gang warfare, pollution and disease. There you find Catholics and Baptists and other evangelical Protestants working together not because they "want to be ecumenical" but because they have to, if they are to be able to say to these people "God loves you like everyone else".

One evening at Casa Materna, a home and social centre run by evangelical Protestants, I was introduced to a man, youngish but looking tired and worn, frightened and lost. He was Polish, and had been found by a Catholic priest who helps migrants and homeless people who turn up on the Naples waterfront. Without papers of any kind, he had probably arrived as a stowaway on a ship: just one of the millions of uprooted people across Europe today. The priest was desperately anxious to find a safe and welcoming place for him while he tried to sort out his legal status before he would be seized and deported. He called Casa Materna, "Can you take this man for two or three nights?" "Sorry, we're absolutely full," was the reply. "But you've *got* to take him," said the priest, "you're the only people who can help him."

When Christians, instead of saying, "We're the only people who can really do any good", and start saying to each other, "You're the only people who can help", then something great and new is coming. And when they say it not for the sake just of a greater church, but for the sake of a hungry and homeless world, then grace and truth are coming. When we give up the ordinary life of self-contentment, and reach for the wine which is the life of Jesus Christ given freely for us all, then strange and new things can happen; and we too can say in wonder, "You have kept the best wine until now." We, like the first disciples, will see his glory, and believe.

Open-door Love

Luke 7:36-38: "One of the Pharisees asked Jesus to eat with him, and he went into the Pharisee's house and took his place at the table. And a woman in the house, who was a sinner... brought an alabaster jar of ointment. She stood behind him at his feet, weeping, and began to bathe his feet with her tears and to dry them with her hair. Then she continued kissing his feet and anointing them with the ointment."

I wonder if any of you have seen the film *Chocolat*. It's set in a small French country town in the 1950s, very set in its ways and where nothing seems to have changed for generations. It's kept under very strict rule by a puritanical mayor, a "buttoned-up" character we would say, and who moreover bludgeons the young Catholic priest into keeping a very strict eye on every aspect of people's behaviour, virtually writing his moralistic sermons for him. Into this scene, seemingly from nowhere, arrives a woman, a single mother with her young daughter. She opens a shop, a chocolate shop. Soon there is chocolate on a scale of abundance unheard of before: chocolate drinks, chocolate sweets, chocolate cakes, chocolate eggs... and all during the season of Lent! The people are by turns surprised, delighted and bewildered... The mayor himself is aghast at this extravagant disruption of order and morality. Where will it end? This woman is a dangerous intruder and she must either change her ways or go, or else there will be chaos. This is only the beginning of a tale, both hilarious and deeply moving, of old ways being upset by a new arrival.

Our gospel reading tells how another woman had a not dissimilar effect on a polite dinner party for theologians held by one Simon, a Pharisee, to which Jesus was invited and came. Before we get into our customary Christian mode of condemning and ridiculing the Pharisees as a whole for being narrow-minded bigots, we should perhaps rather think of Simon as a good, solid and serious-minded citizen of his town, as well as a pillar of the local synagogue. He believed in good order and public integrity, undergirded by a God-fearing moral code. Communities bene-

Sermon preached at Highgate Baptist Church, Birmingham, England, 17 June 2001.

fit from having some such people around and in places of responsibility. They might be resented or laughed at for being "toffee-noses" but they know what duty means. When things go wrong, like a devastating flood or a famine or a foreign invasion, you can depend on it: they will be the ones on hand to hold things together. Every congregation, too, should have at least one Simon!

Anyway, Simon holds a dinner for his like-minded friends and Jesus comes too. As was customary, the door would be left open to the street so that passers-by could see in, take note of who was invited and perhaps be edified by the uplifting religious discussion they could overhear. And in comes this woman... with her gushing emotion, her tearful sobbing and perfumed ointment, literally letting her hair down as she not only throws herself at the feet of Jesus but caresses them with her hands and her hair. The physicality of her embrace verges on the erotic. Simon is shocked, and no doubt some of the others are as well. It's not only what she does, but who she is in his eyes, and the fact that Jesus doesn't seem to mind, that he finds so disturbing. So he has doubts about Jesus: "If this man were a prophet, he would have known who and what kind of woman this is who is touching him – that she is a sinner."

Just as we should not exaggerate Simon's Pharasaic self-righteousness, so we should not for the sake of effect overdraw the woman's reputation. "Sinner" on the lips of a Pharisee would not necessarily have meant that she had led a scandalous sex life, a woman with a story worth selling to the Sunday newspapers, or even that she had once been caught shop-lifting. It may not have meant more than that she didn't belong to the circle of the religiously devout, that she wasn't in the synagogue every sabbath and didn't spend the whole of every day making sure she hadn't transgressed the tiniest detail of the Jewish religious laws and rituals. She, in Simon's eyes, was not "one of us". Whatever the extent of her wrong-doings, great or little, she came from the world outside the purity of the devout, and as "one of them" was likely to be at least a carrier of the virus of sin and impurity.

The outsider has come inside. She has let her hair down and her emotions out, and embraced Jesus in love. Far from this being an intrusion on the dinner party, it becomes the centre-piece of the whole story. Simon has been hoping for some wise words from Jesus, but what Jesus says is quite unexpected. He tells the story of the man who remitted the debts of two people who owed him money, one ten times as much as the other. The one who was forgiven the greatest debt will obviously love the creditor more. So then Jesus speaks gratefully of the woman who has lavished so much affection upon him. "Therefore, I tell you, her sins, which were many, have been forgiven; hence she has shown great love."

Then he pronounces to the woman the forgiveness of her sins, which starts yet another controversy around the table, for who is this who even forgives sins? But Jesus' last word is to the woman herself: "Your faith has saved you; go in peace." Freely she came in through the open door, and even more freely she leaves.

We use a number of different pictures and images for the church. In the Conference of European Churches, as in some other ecumenical bodies, we use as our logo a boat with a cross-shaped mast, riding the waves. That reminds us of the many times the disciples were in a boat with Jesus on Galilee, and also how today we are still with him on the voyage of discipleship and mission, through seas calm or stormy.

But there are other images we could take from the Bible as well. Our gospel reading gives us one such: the meal at the table, in a house with an open door. A place where people meet in fellowship, and which is always open. The church is a space for people to encounter Jesus – in their own way, according to their particular needs and personalities and not according to our prescribed programmes. These days we are often depressed about the way the churches in Europe so often seem marginalized from the life of people and whole societies. But it is also astonishingly true that people do go on finding meaning in Jesus, when the church keeps an open door and allows people to ask their own questions, express their own feelings, and make their own demonstrations of what it means to love and adore the God of forgiving love, like the woman in Simon's house.

Every pastor, looking back over his or her years of ministry, knows of people we think we could have helped more than we did. I recall a mother who didn't belong to the "active" circle of members of the church: she never came to any meetings except the Sunday evening service, and even then not every week. She would not have measured up to Simon's criteria. The reason was, her life and time and energy were consumed in caring for her teenage son who was severely handicapped.

Once when visiting her home I mentioned that we would soon be starting to involve more people in leading our worship services which would then be "livelier" and "more interesting". She leaned back in her chair and with a wistful look in her eye remarked that when she came to church, she just wanted to sit and think. It was about the only time and space in the week she ever had for that. And just before one Christmas, I said I hoped she would be able to be at the carol service. She was not sure, she said: "You see, at Christmas I get so full of emotion, it might all come out." How sad that she felt – maybe correctly and that makes it even sadder – that our fellowship would not be able to allow and accept and cherish tears, as Jesus did.

Church is a place of acceptance where barriers between people come down, and where the door is always open – as yours is in Highgate and where each Sunday you have a fellowship lunch around the table, white and black, young and old, friends and strangers together. There are small communities of faith and open doors just like you, all over Europe. I could show you places in Hamburg, in Amsterdam, in Helsinki, in Naples or in Moscow where you would feel very much at home. Yours and their kind of communities, however small, are the signs of hope that Europe and the wider world need: examples, parables, of accepting space where walls and barriers come down.

And one of our callings as followers of Jesus is not only to keep open the space for people to meet him here, but to recognize where Jesus, even if he is not named or even recognized, is present in the world at large: the one who opens doors, encourages the crossing of boundaries and enables acceptance of one another as sisters and brothers.

One of the most beautiful stories that came out of South Africa during the long struggle against apartheid was about a black township where the mayor was appointed by the government and regarded by most of his neighbours as a stooge. He and his family for many months went in fear of their lives, so much so that their house had to be protected by high barbed-wire fences. Eventually he came to see how things really were, his conscience would not allow him to continue in office any longer and so one day he announced his resignation. That night as he and his family were sitting at home, thinking they would still be very unpopular, and still fearful of what might happen, they heard the sound of people outside and the rending of metal. Terrified, they glimpsed through the curtains. The people were tearing down the barbed-wire. He went outside, thinking that this was the end, only to be greeted by someone calling "Friend, it's OK, you don't need this now!"

As Christians in a world of different faiths and no faith, we need to be able to see Jesus wherever he is recreating and healing life. This last week, we had a meeting near Geneva for religious leaders from the Former Yugoslav Republic of Macedonia. This country has till now been one of the most stable parts of the Balkans even though it is a mix of (mostly) Orthodox Christians, with a large minority of Albanians who are Muslim by faith. But over the past few weeks there have been violent incidents and growing tensions. So this meeting was held for leaders of the Orthodox, Catholic and Methodist churches together with representatives of the Muslim and Jewish communities. It lasted just over 24 hours.

As so often with such encounters, it began with great politeness as everyone present sought to distance themselves and their faith communities from the kind of violence that had taken place. Then the discussion got deeper and more difficult as people began to open up to their real fears: the Christian majority voicing suspicions about the real motives and long-term political aims of the Albanians, the Albanians in turn complaining about being treated as second-class citizens denied their full rights.

But the meeting struggled on, ably chaired by Archbishop Anastasios, the head of the Orthodox Church of Albania, and in the end a very clear and forthright statement was agreed to by all, calling on people of faith to reject violence and establish dialogue. I felt that the most telling moment in the whole meeting came when one of the participants said: "We will get nowhere unless we make the effort to stand in one another's places, and to see ourselves as others see us." That, for me, was Jesus speaking into that situation, for it was such a Christ-like thing to say. But in fact it was said not by one of the Christians present, but by one of the Muslims.

The end of the film *Chocolat* comes on Easter day. Much has happened, hilariously and poignantly, in the meantime. The priest, having now found his own voice instead of being a mouthpiece for the mayor, casts aside his sermon notes and tells the congregation what he has now learnt: that we show our love to God by what we embrace, not by what or whom we exclude. That had been Simon's problem, good as he was. He was so concerned to keep sin out of his house that he was in danger of keeping God out as well. But God did come in. "Do you see this woman?" Jesus asks Simon. He points to her lavish, extravagant loving with tears and perfume pouring over his feet and wiped by her hair. She loves as she is loved.

And perhaps what Jesus is showing Simon, and us, is that while the theologians round the table have been discussing God, and how to keep a safe place for God, she is the one who is providing the picture of God, the God who is lavish, extravagant love, pouring tears over this world and all its people, embracing it in grace and spending everything to the point of a cross.

Middle-aged, Tiring... the Ecumenical Movement Needs a Drink

Psalm 36:9: "For with you is the fountain of life."

I should think there are a number of us here this morning, who can recall the defining moment when it came home to us that we really were now *middle-aged*. For me it was some ten years ago, during a family camping holiday in the Austrian Tirol. Our two sons, then in their late- and mid-teens, reported one afternoon that the camp-site had mountain-bikes for hire and proposed that the three of us should therefore go off mountain-biking. Mother also readily agreed with this guarantee of a peaceful afternoon by herself. So off we went, and it wasn't very long before I realized this venture was a mistake. Not only was the afternoon boiling hot, but I hadn't ridden a bike of any sort anywhere for several years, let alone up and down such steep and stony trails in and out of the forest on the mountainside. In less than an hour I was reduced to a panting grease-spot, sore in one particular part of my anatomy and above all dying of thirst. Eventually we skidded to a halt in a dusty forest clearing. On one side of the clearing was a vertical slab of rock, and out of the rock, sparkling in the sun, was spurting a jet of water. Slow I might have been on the bike, but I was first to that spring. Many drinks of various kinds have I enjoyed in my life, but no chilled lager, no Veuve Cliquot champagne, has ever tasted more heavenly than that pure, ice-cold water straight from the heart of the mountain. I drank, and drank. I placed my head in it, drenched myself in it and began to believe in life again. It was indeed a fountain of life.

Middle-aged, slowing down, short of breath, tired and thirsty: many would say that is a fair description of the ecumenical movement today. For one thing, we hear it said, it doesn't excite people any more. The birth of the modern movement for Christian unity is usually located at the world missionary conference at Edinburgh in 1910, when churches and missionary societies from many parts of the world met to consider how they would work together more closely in the task of bringing the

Sermon preached at Tyndale Baptist church, Bristol, England, 20 January 2002, during the Week of Prayer for Christian Unity.

one gospel to the one world. What made that conference so special was that it didn't just meet and then go away again, but decided to set up a continuation committee to see that its plans were put into practice, a step which proved to be the first on the way to creating the World Council of Churches nearly forty years later. When the proposal was put to the vote after a day of debate, and carried unanimously, the whole assembly spontaneously jumped to its feet and sang the doxology. Excitement! God was doing a new thing! I don't expect many doxologies will be sung this week just because we are having another Week of Prayer for Christian Unity.

Some of us can recall similar excitement even during our own lifetimes. Nearly forty years ago we were agog with the reports that the Second Vatican Council was making pronouncements unheard of and unimaginable before from Rome: about openness to other Christians no longer to be called "separated brethren"; about there being a real if imperfect communion among us all, Catholics or not. As a student in Cambridge I remember a packed congregation one Sunday evening in the university church gathered to hear the abbot of Downside – a leading Catholic – addressing a largely Anglican and Protestant congregation. It seemed that the kingdom of God was just around the corner. But such events are now more or less commonplace, and no longer excite.

Not only do they no longer excite, people are getting a bit cynical about them and ask whether they are really leading us anywhere. The paths are proving very steep and stony. Indeed, we have hit some very big rocks. Less than two years ago a document came out of the Vatican called *Dominus Iesus* which effectively said that Anglican and Protestant churches were not churches in the true sense but only to be called "ecclesial communities". The Catholic bishops of the British Isles have issued a declaration effectively barring Catholics and other Christians from receiving communion together. At the European level where I work, there are even more rocks along our way. Only this week there landed on my desk in Geneva an urgent plea from the bishop of the Methodist Church of Central and Southern Europe, asking me to intervene in Macedonia, a country already riven this past year by ethnic conflict. There, apparently, two Orthodox bishops have been publicly attacking the small Methodist community, claiming it has no place in the country, even though it has been there for many years. A Methodist church building has been vandalized. What makes it even more complicated is that the Orthodox church of Macedonia is itself not even recognized by the other Orthodox churches of Europe as a self-governing church!

Indeed, it has to be confessed that in Europe as a whole in the ten years or so since the fall of the Berlin wall and the dramatic changes in Eastern Europe, the churches have not themselves always presented a very good model of how Europe might truly become a united community of peoples. Resurgent nationalisms in the former Yugoslavia and elsewhere have co-opted religious allegiances onto their agendas. Orthodox East and Catholic West eye each other suspiciously. Pope John Paul visits Greece and the Ukraine, and is hardly welcome by many. Protestant minorities are regarded as interfering proselytizers in the former Soviet Union. And so on.

Middle-aged, tiring, thirsty: where lies our hope? How can excitement and expectancy be re-kindled? If I didn't believe it could be, I suppose I would not be in my present job. But first I would want to say that it is rather unrealistic to imagine that every stage of a journey will be equally exciting. The story of the exodus shows that very clearly. The drama of crossing the Red Sea, the awesomeness of the encounter at Sinai, were fairly short episodes in the long saga of journeying to the Promised Land. God is not only present in the miraculous dividing of the waters and the spectacle of cloud and fire and trumpet blast on the mountain. God also accompanies the day-to-day and year-by-year plod through the desert. Indeed, those are the times when the people are tried and tested to learn the deeper faith that God is with them and for them, and they are to remain faithfully with and for their God. We are called to a steady, realistic faith which does not depend on great dramas and breakthroughs every day.

Then I can go on to say that with such a faith nevertheless comes the expectation of renewal and refreshment. I have to confess a measure of pride about this year's Week of Prayer for Unity, because the material for the prayer and worship has been prepared in Europe, by our Conference of European Churches and the Council of European Bishops Conferences. And I think it is very significant that the joint group which prepared the material selected this text from the Psalms as the theme for the week: "For with you is the fountain of life." The hard experiences we have been going through in the European churches have been teaching us that the search for a deeper and closer unity involves more than negotiation over doctrinal differences, more than agreeing how to reconcile different views of ministry and church order and the sacraments, more even than cooperating on meeting human need and on missionary outreach. Something deeper is needed: a new contact with God, with God's own life as made known in Jesus Christ in the power of the Holy Spirit.

Christian unity is not just about reorganizing the church so that it might perform its task better (though it is). Christian unity is not just about enabling Christians and churches to present an example to the world of how God wants the world to be, reconciled and at peace (though it most certainly is that). At heart, it is about letting the world see who *God* is, the one God who loves all he has made and gave all he had in Jesus; the God who in his steadfast and precious love is the one fountain of life for all people and all creation, the one fountain where all are welcome to drink. Christian unity is about letting God renew us and remake us as a community, not excluding but mutually embracing, as God has embraced us on the cross; not holding one another's faults and failings against each other but accepting and forgiving as God in Christ has forgiven us; not seeking to dominate and pontificate over against each other, but learning from and sharing with each other, with the humility of Jesus the servant who placed a child as an example in the midst of his disciples; not laying down the written law but living in the freedom of the Spirit, by whom the love of God is shared among us all. It is about what Archbishop Rowan Williams calls "a shared passion" which recognizes "not just a need to understand each other and to be able politely to work and even worship alongside each other, but a need to *understand God together*": a shared passion based on the wonder of our incorporation into the triune life of God in Christ.

"For with you is the fountain of life." There is where we need to go, to the one refreshing source of life which is God's own self, to drink and be drenched in it. Here are some more recent words from Europe: "Ecumenism therefore begins for Christians with the renewal of our hearts and the willingness to repent and change our ways." They come from the "Charta Oecumenica" which was launched at a gathering in Strasbourg, France, just after Easter 2001. In the Conference of European Churches and the Council of European Bishops Conferences we had decided that we would celebrate the first Easter of the new millennium in a special way, by bringing together in Strasbourg – from all over Europe, east and west, north and south – one hundred leaders of all kinds of churches – Protestant, Anglican, Orthodox, Free Church and so on. And not only church leaders – bishops, cardinals and the like – but also an equal number of young people: again, from all confessions and all parts of Europe.

It was an encounter not only between the various Christian traditions but between the generations too. A good antidote to the ecumenical movement succumbing to middle-age spread. They came to pray together, to study the Bible together, to share together in very personal ways what their faith means to them and their vision for the future of the gospel in Europe. I could tell many stories from those few days together. But no time was more moving than an afternoon in the Council of

Europe building, when a series of church leaders and young people gave their own testimonies of faith and the way they wanted it expressed in Europe today. Those of us who were there will never forget the young man from Romania who had come to faith in Christ only two or three years previously, and who presented the gathering with a pair of sandals as a symbol of his commitment to continue walking the way of faith come what may. And on the other hand, Cardinal Etchegaray of France, one of the most senior Roman Catholics present, who told very simply how every time he goes to the altar to celebrate communion he feels he should not be there and it is a only sense of God's grace which keeps him from running away. It is meeting at that level, where we all admit our tiredness and thirst and realize that we have to drink from the same fountain of life, that the journey towards unity is renewed.

But to come back to those words I just quoted: "Ecumenism... begins for Christians with the renewal of our hearts and the willingness to repent and change our ways." The "Charta Oecumenica" is a setting out of commitments for how the European churches should behave towards each other, and of their common responsibilities towards Europe, a Europe of justice and peace, a Europe of diverse yet reconciled peoples and cultures, a Europe where people of different religions now live yet a Europe where the rights of all must be respected. It is now being studied and discussed all over Europe and has aroused great interest, and is even creating ripples in other parts of the world (though I have to say I have heard some rather smug comments from Britain to the effect that "we don't really need it here"). It is about the need for change and transformation at every level of our church life, whichever denomination we belong to, and about transforming the life of Europe. And it begins with this affirmation that the change has to begin with each of us.

For the greatest barrier to unity is our sense of self-sufficiency, the assumption that whether as individuals or churches or nations we are OK as we are, left as we are. But if we drink from and are drenched in the fountain of life which is God's own life, we shall be transformed, brought out of our old satisfaction with ourselves into the endlessly enriching life of the God who is boundless and gracious love, love which rejoices in being with and for others, love which is not content with isolation but exults in community, just as God's own eternal and blessed life is a life of endless love, three-in-one and one-in-three, the communion of Father, Son and Holy Spirit. Christian unity is about letting that love-in-communion be seen in the life of God's people.

That is what it comes down to. For too long in the ecumenical movement we have made complacent assumptions: that we already know enough about God, and Christian unity is simply about rearranging the pattern of the church. Maybe, through our middle-aged exhaustion, God has been teaching us that we have to begin again by learning who God is, by asking the simple but dangerous questions: who Jesus Christ is for us today, what a cross and resurrection and a Pentecost will mean for us today – and only then begin to understand what it means to be the church of God, a community which reflects the God who is cross-shaped love. We have to pause, and drink from the sparkling fountain-head.

So – middle-aged, tiring, thirsty? Maybe. But springs are flowing. People are drinking, Protestant, Catholic, Orthodox, Pentecostal, who-ever. And if it is the one fountain of life, to which all are welcome, that they are drinking from, who can tell what might happen in the future? I have to confess that, like some novels and some films, this sermon has two alternative endings. It could be that the future is one of continual hard pedalling, but continually refreshed by that spring which is the never-ending outpouring of the Holy Spirit. We shall reach the goal by a combination of devoted study of the issues that separate us, by ever-deepening persistence in doing together what we can do together until we realize we are doing everything together. That is one scenario. It might well be like that.

On the other hand, who can predict what might happen if renewal and repentance and changing of ways really start to work in people's lives? What might be the outcome of that "shared passion" which comes out of a new understanding of God together, a new understanding which is born out of a deeper immersion, a deeper baptism, into Christ himself in the Spirit? If we cannot wholly foresee it, neither will we be able wholly to control it, whether in our church structures or our ecumenical organiza-tions. As general secretary of one such body, I am called various things from time to time. I am relieved to say that the title "prophet" is not nor-mally accorded me. So I will not dare to prophesy, but just admit to a hunch.

I have a hunch that in the life-time of many of us here, a new advance, a new breakthrough, will occur. I don't know quite where, or precisely when. But I suspect that if and when it comes, it will come not so much through carefully negotiated agreements and cautiously planned restructuring, but rather through the people of Christ at large saying, "Enough is enough. We are going to be together at the Lord's table, we are going to recognize all baptized Christians as members of one body, and their ministers as our ministers of Christ to us, and what-ever we've been doing separately we are going to do together." The pow-ers that be in some of the churches may not like it, they will say that it is theologically inadmissible and ecclesiastically not allowable. But, just like the first church in Jerusalem worrying over the gentiles coming to faith, they will have to learn to revise their doctrine in the light of what the Spirit is actually doing to make the love of Christ visible and known in the world.

There will be protests. May there also, and louder, be doxologies. You cannot stop the fountain of life flowing, and it is in God's light that we shall see light.

After 11 September – a New Creation?

2 Corinthians 5:14-21, v.17: "So if anyone is in Christ, there is a new creation: everything old has passed away; see, everything has become new!"

Sarajevo! For those of us who are visitors here, this is a very special experience. We are in the city whose name just a few years ago meant – to all of us in Europe – conflict, suffering, violence, brutality, yet also courage, endurance, patience and an unquenchable faith in the eventual triumph of humanity. Sarajevo is also a name which, over a longer time-span, has been etched in the minds of European people as the place where, in 1914, was ignited the conflict which plunged the whole of Europe into war and, some would say, really inaugurated the 20th century as the era of violence. But this Sunday morning, here in this church, it is also for us a place of warm welcome and fellowship, and vibrant worship. For those of us who have spent the past few days deep in intensive study and long discussions, it is certainly a welcome change to come and share in joyful prayer and fervent singing!

Not that we have not enjoyed our conference or found it important. Far from it. It has been enriching, to meet not only with other Christians – Protestants, Catholics and Orthodox – from all over Europe but with Muslims too. The meeting was planned long ago, to bring together for the first time at a European level Christian and Muslim representatives to consider their common responsibilities in today's European society. We chose Sarajevo as the venue because, as perhaps nowhere else in Europe, here is symbolized the need for communities of different faiths to be able to live together, to receive healing and reconciliation.

But what none of us could have anticipated was how tragically significant this particular week would prove to be. Many of our participants were already travelling on 11 September, and not until the next day on their arrival here did they feel the full impact of the news of the terrible events in New York and elsewhere in the United States. How strange that

---

Sermon preached in Sarajevo Baptist church, 16 September 2001, following the Conference of European Churches-Council of European Bishops Conferences Christian-Muslim conference on "Christians and Muslims in a Pluralist Europe".

such a meeting as this between Christians and Muslims should coincide with the immediate aftermath of the terrorist attacks in New York and Washington, attacks which many are already feeling may have some religious element in them. Strange – or dare we say it might prove to be providential? At any rate, it has lent a completely unforeseen depth of seriousness to our encounters and discussions, and not just in the way it prompted us all, Christians and Muslims alike, as our first reaction to make a common declaration condemning such acts as flagrant contradictions of God's will for peace and respect for human life.

And perhaps you here in Sarajevo, who for many long days experienced what it was like to be under attack, and maybe also knew the loss of loved ones and neighbours, felt a special closeness to the victims and their families. We do not know, yet, what will be the full consequences of the events of last Tuesday. But many of us feel that somehow we have crossed a threshold into a different and very unfamiliar world; a boundary has been crossed which we never dreamt could be violated on such a scale, and how the international community will handle it remains completely unknown. Life is always uncertain – but now as never before.

At such a time, what is our response as Christians to be? At first, of course, it is a kind of baffled helplessness such as we share with all people. But even then, it matters that we bring our baffled helplessness to God. When the news broke on us on Tuesday afternoon in the office of CEC in Geneva, both the least and the most we thought we could do was to e-mail a short message of solidarity and sympathy to our sisters and brothers in the National Council of Churches in the USA, with the prayer that we might all now be given the strength and wisdom to remain faithful to Christ and witnesses to peace in the midst of violence.

Just *how* we are to be such witnesses in these days we still have to discover. But the point of such a prayer is that it places us, here and now, in all our uncertainty, at the disposal of God. Prayer is the way in which we turn the place where we are standing, even if it is at the moment in darkness, into the place where heaven's light can eventually fall. Prayer turns sheer paralysis into waiting in hope. Earlier in this service we heard the young people singing a song, the tune of which I know and the words – if it is the same song as in English – are about God leading us by the hand. At such a time as this, we acknowledge that we do need to be led, and will be led.

It is with all this in mind that I turn to our scripture reading, 2 Corinthians 5:14-21, and especially Paul's words in verse 17: *So if anyone is in Christ, there is a new creation; everything old has passed away; see, everything has become new!*

As I said, with the events of 11 September many of us feel we are now in a very different and unfamiliar world. In a rather odd way, perhaps that helps us hear more clearly the message of Paul here: "everything old has passed away..." Something new and unfamiliar is here. Not a threatening world but nevertheless strange and unfamiliar according to the standards and outlook of the world we are used to. Paul is saying that Jesus has brought an entirely *new creation* into being. Not, of course, through anything like a violent terrorist act but on the contrary through his suffering a cruelly violent death upon the cross and being raised to life again. Because of Jesus nothing can ever be the same again, says Paul. He died for all, therefore all people are to be looked upon in a new way, God's way, the way of God's love which wants the world to be reconciled to himself. So when we are joined to Jesus by our faith in him, we enter a new world, we cross a boundary to where everything and everyone looks different. There is a new creation, everything old has passed away, everything has become new. It is not so much that those who follow Jesus are supposed to be "better" than others. It is simply that once we are conscious of living in the sphere of God's love for us and for all people, everything is *different, new*.

If this is so, then strange and unexpected things can happen, right now in the real world we live in. But "peace" and "reconciliation" – are they just dream-words, which we often talk about too easily and glibly? They can be, and right now perhaps we are tempted to feel that is all they are, and leave them on the page of the letter Paul wrote to the Corinthians. But they have also been written in the lives of real people.

Let me share with you one story of such people, which is very simple but to which I always turn to refresh my hope. It is one I think about increasingly over the years. Over thirty years ago I left theological seminary and university to begin my ministry in a small Baptist congregation in the north of England. Of course, I thought I knew just about everything and it was my job to teach the people. I soon found that not everyone was interested in what I thought I had to preach and teach. What was more, some had a lot to teach me.

Especially, there was one couple nearing retirement age called Harold and Amy. They were very down-to-earth, working people – Harold was a painter at the big chemical works down the hill from the village – and I saw very few books in their home. Harold had a face like crumpled steel but beneath that hard-bitten look lay something else, and from him and Amy I learnt something which I have been trying to understand ever since. For they had a special story, which I heard several times from other people and once from Harold himself one cold and snowy morning as we waited outside the chapel for some workmen to arrive for a repair job on the building. He told it to me, after all those years, still with a sense almost of wondering disbelief that it could have happened.

Harold and Amy had had two sons. The older one was killed in the second world war. He was a naval airman and was lost in an attack on the huge German battleship, the *Tirpitz*. When the dreaded news came, Harold was so smitten with grief and rage, he swore that the first German he met he would break his neck, and in that bitterness he remained. In May 1945 the war in Europe ended. Shortly afterwards there took place in the village an event which for a Baptist chapel in the north of England is very important – the annual Sunday school anniversary when the afternoon service would largely be occupied by the children singing, reciting poems and so on. Harold was standing outside the chapel as the children and their fond parents, grandparents and friends and relations were arriving. Then two young men came up, dressed in drab grey uniforms. Diffidently, and in broken English, they asked what was happening? "Sunday School anniversary," said Harold, "Children – lots of singing! Come on in!" An instant later, Harold realized what he had done. He had broken his vow. He had met his first Germans – prisoners of war from the nearby camp and now allowed out a few hours each day – and instead of breaking their necks he had invited them into his church.

The two young Germans came back to the chapel one evening the following week, with several more of their mates from the camp, and joined in table-tennis and other games at the youth club. And not many days later, the news was going round the village: that Harold and Amy were the first people to have these German lads round to tea at their house, sitting at the same table where their own dear son was so sorely missed. It was no passing friendship, but developed into a deep and long-standing one. One of the prisoners, Sigmund by name, in fact came from a Baptist church in the Ruhr, and between his family and Harold's and Amy's the friendship continued long after Sigmund and the others had returned home, right down to their respective grandchildren. Just before I left that pastorate, we opened a new chapel building, and from the pastor of Sigmund's church came a special greeting card including our text: "If anyone is in Christ, there is a new creation." So indeed there is, and the most extraordinary things can happen in the lives of so-called ordinary people.

Indeed, what Paul is effectively saying in our Bible passage is that after Jesus no one is ordinary any more. It is this belief in the meaning of Jesus and the transforming effect of the love seen in him that we are called to work out in all our relationships. Healing and reconciling love shape the strange new world, the new creation, we live in by our faith. No violence, no act of destruction however terrible, must be allowed to shake us out of this new creation in Christ. Indeed, such events leave us nowhere else to go. Barely 24 hours after the attack on the World Trade Center and the Pentagon, I received an e-mail from a friend in the USA, a short meditation he was sending around to friends and colleagues in America and all over the world, based on words of St Augustine: "Whoever does not serve love, serves evil." In the midst of the shock and devastation wrought by the forces of this old world, and fearing the forces of revenge, he was determined to live – even then – in the new creation. May we all serve that love, and pray to be part of that love, in the coming days.

Staying with Christ

John 6:67f.: "So Jesus also asked the twelve, 'Do you also wish to go away?' Simon Peter answered him, 'Lord, to whom can we go? You have the words of eternal life.'"

Dear sisters and brothers in Christ:

I cannot tell you what a joy it is to be with you in Georgia at last. Over the past three or four years I have felt a little like the apostle Paul when he wrote to the Christians in Rome and told them, "that I have often intended to come to you but thus far have been prevented", and I pray, like Paul "that we may be mutually encouraged by each other's faith, both yours and mine". There is at least this difference between Paul and myself, that I have come to Tbilisi not as a prisoner but as a very welcome guest, and with deepest gratitude I thank Bishop Malkhaz and the Baptist community, and the other churches, for their welcome, their hospitality, and their readiness to share with me their experience, their hopes and concerns, for Christian life and witness in this beautiful country of Georgia.

I want to bring you assurance that you are remembered by us in the Conference of European Churches, along with churches and Christians all over the world. We have been following very closely events in Georgia, and adding our voice of concern and advocacy on your behalf, following the disturbing experiences you have been going through. Let me say then very clearly what we believe in CEC: in the Europe of today, respect for human rights and the upholding of the rule of law must be the duty of every government – there can be no exceptions. The Conference of European Churches, which works closely with the Council of Europe and the Organization for Security and Cooperation in Europe, will continually advocate this.

The other day in Geneva, I was speaking to someone about my visit here, and he said half jokingly, "Why on earth would anyone want to visit Georgia?" He was no doubt thinking of all the problems which

Sermon preached at an ecumenical service in Central Baptist Church, Tbilisi, Georgia, 26 June 2002.

Georgia has in these days, and the fact that visitors are not always welcomed in some quarters. I replied, "Because I've been invited." But one of the reasons I am glad to be here is precisely because it is in places where there are great problems and difficulties that great truths are discovered about what the church of Jesus Christ is for, about what the meaning of the gospel is for us today. And I am eager to learn from you what you are finding out of the purposes of God for his people today, so that I may be able to return to Geneva and share this with your sisters and brothers in the wider Christian family.

So it is moving to be in this great historic nation of Europe, where the Christian faith has been proclaimed and lived for so many centuries, ever since that slave-girl from Cappadocia, Nina, first dared to speak the name of Jesus here in the 4th century. But in talking with people from Georgia, and who have visited Georgia in recent years, and in reading about the churches in Georgia, several times I have come across one phrase which sums up how Georgian Christians, whether Baptist or Orthodox or whatever, feel at the moment. I hear them saying, "We are at a new beginning." After more than fifty years of atheist communist rule when the churches suffered so appallingly, after the upheavals of ten years ago, in the midst of terrible economic conditions and political uncertainties, people feel that in both church and society they have to make a new start, a new start with so few resources. A new start where the outside world has not always been helpful to them.

As a West European I must confess with some shame that while we were glad to see the end of the old communist empire we did not match that gladness with enough real aid and encouragement to assist countries like Georgia in their new beginning. But as Christians we know that the most important basis for a new beginning is our faith in God as revealed to us in Jesus Christ in the power of the Holy Spirit. That, very simply, is what I wish to share with you this evening, as we turn to the word of God as we have heard it read in holy scripture.

Our text comes from John's gospel, at a moment of crisis in the ministry of Jesus. Crowds of people have been eagerly coming to Jesus, the great miracle worker who has wondrously fed them with bread in the wilderness. But then he tells them that the most important bread is not that which is baked in an oven, but he himself, the bread of life. That it is in following him, one who is going to die and be raised again, that true life is found. That it is in total surrender to him, total union with him, to death and beyond death, that life is found. That it is in accepting him who gives his life to us on a cross, and sharing that cross, that we come to know God and life in God. That is too much for many of the people. From being a popular preacher, Jesus now becomes a dangerous, controversial figure, and people start to leave him. So Jesus looks round at his twelve disciples and says, "Will you also go away?" And Peter says, "Lord, to whom shall we go? You have the words of eternal life."

To whom shall we go? To whom shall we go in a difficult time when old certainties are gone and yet we cannot see the way ahead? To whom shall we go when we are beset by so many problems in our lives, our personal lives, our family life, our life as a nation, our lives as churches? To whom shall we go when we are criticized, mocked, threatened, or even treated violently and shamefully by people who call us heretics, or traitors to our nation? This is not the first time that the people of God have asked this question, and it will not be the last. The Christian community has lived through twenty centuries, and it will live till God's kingdom comes in power and glory, because of those who again and again see that they must simply stay with Jesus himself, the one who has the words of eternal life.

People sometimes ask me why I, as a Baptist, am also an ecumenist. They think that Baptists are narrow-minded sectarians who reckon that their way is the one and only true Christian way. I thank God for my Baptist upbringing and thank God that by his grace I was called to be a Baptist pastor. I believe that there are great and precious truths that God has made known to us as Baptists: that his saving word is found in scripture, that the church is the gathered fellowship of believers, that baptism by immersion in water on profession of repentance and faith in Christ is the way of union with Christ and entry into his church. But the most fundamental tenet of Baptist belief is the sole lordship of Christ himself. The living Lord Jesus Christ himself is the Lord of the church, the company of believers, and no earthly power can come between him and his people. The living Christ himself is the lord of our lives, our conscience, our souls and bodies.

If I believe that, if I believe that Jesus Christ is the supreme reality to whom all authority in heaven and on earth is given, then I have to confess that while he owns me, I do not own him like a private possession, like my car or TV set, or have him under my control. He is Lord over me, not I over him. He is wherever he makes himself known by his power and his grace. I therefore have to look to wherever else he is acknowledged as Lord and Saviour among all his people, of whatever confession or tradition. I have to learn more of him through others who are learning of him in ways different to my own. I cannot love and serve Christ without seeking him among and with all his followers.

It is rather like having a friend. I have a great friend in my life. His name is Christopher – his name means "Christ-bearer" after the story of the saint who without knowing it carried the Christ-child across a dangerous river. And Christopher is certainly one who helped carry Christ into my own life. We were students together at Cambridge, which is where we became such close friends. We walked together, visited each other's homes, went on camping holidays together. On a very special day in my life, our wedding day, he stood beside me as my "best man". Over the years we have remained good friends, but of course have not seen quite so much of each other. I became a pastor, Christopher became a schoolteacher, eventually headmaster of a school.

A few years ago, it was Christopher's 50th birthday and his wife and family organized a party for him. It was a wonderful evening, there were crowds of people there, some whom we knew from old days, but many we had not met before. We shared our stories of what Christopher meant to us. For me, he was still the old student friend. But others knew him in ways I didn't: those who had been in his colleagues in various schools, those who had been his next-door neighbours. The same Christopher, but known in more ways than any single one of us could know. I think of the ecumenical movement as rather like that. We come together out of love for Christ, not in order to be exactly like each other or to impose our own understanding on each other, but to share our experience and vision of who Jesus is for us, so that the world might see we are one in him, and the world might believe.

"Lord, to whom else shall we go? You have the words of eternal life." It is our undying friendship with Christ himself that we must continually recover as the church of God. That is why I thank God for the Orthodox church, because of all churches the Orthodox have continually reminded us of the historic confession of faith which has Jesus Christ as Son of God at its centre. In the words of the great Nicene-Constantinopolitan ecumenical creed of the 4th century: "We believe in one Lord Jesus Christ, the only begotten Son of God, begotten of the Father before all worlds, God from God, light from light, begotten, not made, of one being with the Father, by whom all things were made, who for us and for our salvation came down from heaven, and was incarnate by the Holy Spirit of the Virgin Mary and was made man..." That is the Christ by whom we must stay if we are to have a faith which withstands all opposition and which is to be a message for our world.

I thank God that continually down the years the lordship of Christ has been rediscovered and brought out afresh. When Martin Luther in the 16th century sought to restore belief solely in the grace of God as the means of our salvation, it was a rediscovery of Jesus Christ. At the top of the first page of all his writings and sermons he wrote the name "Jesus". I thank God for those Protestant Christians in Nazi Germany in the 1930s who resisted the Nazi attempt to make a substitute religion of race, blood and soil and to place loyalty to Adolf Hitler above everything else. In 1934, at a place called Barmen, they issued a declaration which recalled their church to its real belief: "Jesus Christ, as he is testified to us in holy scripture, is the one Word of God which we are to hear, which we are to trust and obey in life and in death. We repudiate the false teachings that the church can and must recognize yet other happenings and powers, personalities and truths as divine revelation alongside this one word of God, as a source of her preaching."

And, in all humility, I dare to thank God for our own Conference of European Churches. In June 2003, at Trondheim in Norway, we shall be having our 12th general assembly. And the theme for that assembly, chosen by our central committee, is "Jesus Christ Heals and Reconciles – Our Witness in Europe". Jesus Christ heals and reconciles: strange it may seem, but this is the first time in the forty years of CEC's life that for an assembly theme Jesus Christ is named so explicitly and clearly, and right at the beginning of the title. Perhaps that too is a sign that in the ecumenical movement itself we are recognizing that if we wish God to renew us and give us a new beginning, a new future, we have nowhere else to go but to Jesus Christ himself, and his healing and reconciling work.

We have much to thank God for in Europe. It is a great part of the world in which to live. But Europe today also cries out for healing. There are wounded memories of past conflicts which still embitter people, still create mistrust and suspicion. There are actual ongoing conflicts today: violence and bloodshed so close to here, in Chechnya, or far away in Spain. There is a sickness of inhumanity in Europe, as people in search of jobs and a better life arrive in Western Europe and meet with racial hostility; as women and girls are trafficked from East to West Europe and end up in sexual slavery. There is actual sickness abroad as HIV-AIDS spreads in many parts of Europe. There is a feeling of lostness for many people, both in East and West, who feel betrayed by the collapse of the old socialist ideology but are offered no hope by the forces of globalizing capitalism, which treat people merely as expendable workers or consumers, but with no real control over their own lives.

In face of all this, to whom shall we go but Jesus Christ, with his gospel of healing and reconciliation? To whom shall we go for the good news that human beings, each and every man, woman and child, are beloved children of God and therefore deserving of dignity, respect and freedom? To whom shall we go for the good news that no one is to be written off as useless but intended for fullness of life now and hereafter?

To whom shall we go for the good news that broken relationships can be mended, that enemies can become friends again, that peace is a real promise? To whom shall we go that even our worst sins are not the last word about us, but that there is forgiveness, healing, new life available for each? To whom shall we go for the good news that none of us need be left out and alone, that there is community of love, forgiven and forgiving? To whom shall we go, but to Jesus who has the words of eternal life, hope and peace?

Perhaps I am speaking to someone this evening who says, "It's fine for you to talk about Europe – but what about me? My life's in a mess. I'm overwhelmed with problems. I don't know where to turn, or whom to turn to. I feel I don't count. I wish I was dead." Friend, I say to you: Of course I do not know all you are going through. But I do know there are others present who have felt as you do now. They have felt loneliness, pain, bitterness and despair. They too have felt life had no meaning or purpose. But they discovered this one called Jesus, who makes us see life, ourselves and everything else differently. He wants to come to us with his love. Moreover, he wants to live his life of love in us and through us. You too can make this discovery. Ask him, and you will find him already closer to you than you expect.

Friends, you will know, more than I, that Georgia itself cries out for healing and reconciliation. And some of you know that it can be very hard to speak of healing and reconciliation when you face intolerance and fanaticism, especially when they take religious forms. That is one of the most tragic and dangerous features of our world today, made more so since 11 September last year. To whom else can we go when people abuse us, attack us, even burn our Bibles? When such things happen, the experience of the people of God down the years can inspire us.

We need not lose hope. For 13 years I taught in our Baptist seminary in Bristol, England, the oldest Baptist seminary in the world. At that time, we had a famous collection of historic Bibles. Most precious of all was one small New Testament. It was the only surviving complete copy of the first printed English New Testament, made by William Tyndale in 1525. What happened to all the rest? They were burnt by order of the king of England and the bishops of the church who at that time did not want people to read the Bible in their own tongue. A few years later Tyndale himself was put to death. His final words as he faced death were, "Lord, open the king of England's eyes!" Not long after, the king's eyes *were* opened, and Bibles in English were found not only in every church but countless homes too. God does open people's eyes. That is our hope.

That is easy for me to say, an outsider who will in a couple of days be safely on a plane back to Geneva. But the most important thing to say is that those who stay with Christ can never be defeated, in life or in death. He is the Lord, the bringer of eternal life. He was put to death, and raised to life, and sends us his Spirit. He knows what it means to take risks, he knows what danger is, he knows what suffering is, he knows what death is. He is greater than all risks, greater than all danger, greater than all suffering, greater even than death, for he is the one who died and is the living one. He has the words of eternal life, for he *is himself* the word of eternal life. Stay with him.